D1644713

TRADING SECRETS:

Rod Gilmour

TRADING SECRETS:

SQUASH GREATS RECALL THEIR GREATEST DUELS

Foreword by
Malcolm Willstrop

First published by Pitch Publishing, 2015

Pitch Publishing
A2 Yeoman Gate
Yeoman Way
Durrington
BN13 3QZ
www.pitchpublishing.co.uk

A CIP catalogue record is available for this book
from the British Library.

ISBN 978-178531-043-0

Typesetting and origination by Pitch Publishing

Printed in Great Britain by Bell and Bain Ltd, Glasgow

Contents

Acknowledgments

THE FOLLOWING have all played an instrumental part in how this book was put together. Ian McKenzie, *Squash Player Magazine*'s editor, for letting me into his archives and reproduction of articles, Howard Harding for statistics, Richard Eaton and Andrew Shelley for their expertise and photographer Steve Line. I also recommend a subscription to *Squash Player Magazine* at www.squashplayer.co.uk/subscriptions.

ROD GILMOUR has covered squash for the *Daily Telegraph* and *Squash Player Magazine* since 2008. He collaborated with James Willstrop on his diaries for *Shot and a Ghost: a year in the brutal world of professional squash*, which was nominated for the prestigious William Hill Sports Book of the Year award in 2012.

Foreword By Malcolm Willstrop

MY FIRST experience of the game of squash came in my schooldays at St Peter's York, which had a tradition of squash through England cricket captain Norman Yardley, winner of the North of England men's title three times, I believe, while still a pupil, W. Toyne, headmaster and formerly of Haileybury College and Gerald Pawle, contemporary of Yardley's and a *Daily Telegraph* sports writer.

The court was a converted Fives court at the side of the cricket field and the queues to book the court were always long! Little did I realise that one day I would be watching players I coach playing at world level under the Pyramids, in New York's Grand Central Station and by Hong Kong Harbour – all quite wonderful locations to play squash.

I remember being on a three-day course at Uxbridge to see if I was suitable officer material in the RAF. I told the panel that I was a squash player and how impressed they were – not by me but by the game.

Those were the days of courts in the Officers Mess, private clubs, which still exist, and the public schools.

The best players in those days came from Oxbridge: Jonny Leslie (Rugby), John Easter (St Edward's), Phil Ayton (Brighton College or Lancing), Kim Bruce Lockhart (Harrow), who sadly died young. The dominant schools then were Lancing, Barnard Castle and Gresham's.

Those were the days of the Lansdowne and the RAC clubs. When I went back to teach at St Peter's, two new courts had been built, the game was taking off and along came Jonah Barrington, which was just what the sport needed. He rightly caught the attention of the media, released the game from its conservative fetters and the boom was on.

We sometimes forget just how far the game has progressed in such a short time. Who would have predicted the glass court, the spectacular venues all over the world, the world tour? I remember, too many moons ago, going to a hangar in Blackpool to test the perspex court.

That was an amazing experience. I was there at the first unofficial World Junior Championship in the cold of Sundsvall, Sweden. I was there years later to see my son, James, win his title in Chennai. This after my other son, Christy, came third, stepson David Campion had come second, so it took three goes.

There have been the greats: Jahangir Khan, Jansher Khan, Jonah, Geoff Hunt, Peter Nicol, Amr Shabana and the most original player ever to have lived, Ramy Ashour.

But the depth of the professional game nowadays is plain to see and with it we have enjoyed the era of Shabana, Nick Matthew, Ashour, Willstrop, Greg

Gaultier and Karim Darwish: the strongest ever crop at the top of the game.

As it now enters change, it is unlikely to be replicated, at least immediately. Shabana was and is complete, Ashour is a genius, Matthew a great achiever and there is much to admire with the other three too.

The game at the top provides a living, but hardly reflects the quality of the players and the severe demands of the game.

It had early problems with television, which was long ago solved by PSA TV and its production output. The men's final at the Commonwealth Games in Glasgow was a powerful showpiece, but the game has not been glamorised enough and hasn't yet realised how vital betting is to attract media attention.

Yet, the progress the game has made is remarkable. I hope that in the next few years the professionals will be properly rewarded for their skills, hard work and resilience. Few sportsmen work so hard for their living. Hopefully there is more to come.

MALCOLM WILLSTROP is one of the most respected coaches in the history of the game. He was recognised for his services to the sport when he was inducted into the UK Sport coaching hall of fame in 2004. He has coached for over 50 years and, for over two decades, at Pontefract Squash Club where he took son, James, and Lee Beachill to the world No.1 position.

Introduction

REPORTING ON squash is an odd concept. From an outsiders' point of view, it may be played in small confines, with two players thrashing a ball against a wall and not much else to go on, but squash is so much more than that.

It is one of the most consistently draining sports I have covered as a journalist. Watching two athletes battle it out in a small glass box from close quarters, you feel part of the action. You *are* one of those players. Throw in a two-hour, five-game marathon and you can come away with your energy sapped. It is intoxicating and, more often than not at the top of the game, dramatic.

This is certainly the case at an event such as the Tournament of Champions at Grand Central Terminal in New York. The press area is situated underneath the stands behind the back wall in the art deco Vanderbilt Hall and, in between matches, you brush past players trying to warm up in the small areas consigned to the event. There's a buzz like no other, while the ToC encapsulates the sport as a whole: cover squash long enough and you bear witness to player habits, the moods, the freneticism. Squash simply sucks you in.

The stories and subplots surrounding tournaments or individual matches are endlessly fascinating too. In essence, it is all about the match-ups and rivalries, the pursuit of beating the best at the time, the fight to get into the top 16 where life as a touring professional starts to bear fruit.

So, rather than reading about these specific matches and points as a whole, and how these greats won the titles, my aim was to get a clearer picture of their thoughts and mindsets at the time and how they were able to cross the winning line (unless your name is the indefatigable and unbeatable Jahangir Khan).

Back in the heyday of squash – the late 1960s to the late 80s, when clubs were flourishing, the sport found a regular spot on BBC's *Grandstand* and reports were regular fodder for sports editors – press rooms were a lively place to be.

Unfortunately, those media coverage good times have dwindled as the sport has progressed to the thrill it is today: modern glass courts, a high-definition TV product and remarkably fit entertainers few know about (Olympian Jessica Ennis told me in 2012 that Nick Matthew, Yorkshire's three-time world champion, was Britain's most understated and fittest sportsman).

Yet, the stories are still bountiful. British journalists attending the 2014 Commonwealth Games in Glasgow will testify to that, having crossed Glasgow to Scotstoun to watch the final between James Willstrop and Matthew and made reference to the pair's career-long, lively rivalry in their reports.

The press tribunes were packed with a representative from every UK newspaper and major news agency that day. Even though it took an all-English final on a Monday to do so, it showed that squash is not a low-end 'general sport'. It deserves the right to be reported on as any major sport would: player reactions, match reports, analysis or evocative pictures sitting alongside. That will hopefully change to some degree when squash is finally admitted into the Olympics, though the sport still seeks the nod from the International Olympic Committee after three fraught and fruitless bid campaigns attempting to swoon IOC chiefs in recent years.

The World Squash Federation's bid for inclusion to the London 2012 Games was curtailed by a controversial two-thirds majority vote by the IOC's executive committee which saw no sport included, despite squash and karate doing enough to warrant a place.

Four years later, rugby sevens and golf were given preferential treatment for inclusion to the 2016 Rio Games. For the 2020 bid, squash spent a reported £1m and put together the best showcase of the sport's portrayal yet.

The signs looked good. Wrestling, one of the most traditional of Olympic sports, was cut from the Games programme before a last-minute reprieve by the IOC saw the ancient sport put back into the frame for Tokyo. Squash was then left on its knees as the doors of the IOC session in Buenos Aires were thrust open and wrestling rejoiced in the Hilton Hotel basement lobby. It is an image that will stay with me until the sport is finally accepted in.

The IOC suits had scuppered squash's ambition once more. But there was respite in the form of new

IOC president, Thomas Bach, who immediately set about changing the make-up of future Olympics thanks to the German's flexible approach (who had taken over from Jacques Rogge, and who incidentally had a penchant for rugby, having played for Belgium). At the time of writing, Tokyo 2020 hopes remain alive as the IOC charter is rewritten to accommodate Bach's raft of reforms.

For now, squash is showing signs of emerging from two decades sat in a motionless bubble. Players continue to traipse around the world largely unnoticed, promoters continue to put on events, but the commercial side of the sport is showing resurgence as sponsors latch on to the sport's potential at staging events in glamorous locations. January 2015 was also a landmark date for world squash, with the men's and women's tours having merged.

Meanwhile, stories of past glories live on. At each major event, I am usually regaled with yarns by the remaining stalwarts in the media room – *Agence France Presse*'s Richard Eaton, long-time photographer Steve Line, *Squash Player* editor Ian McKenzie, squash's long-serving media man Howard Harding, and Alan Thatcher. Hence, this book has been borne out of conversations with the aforementioned names on some of the past players and characters to have graced this great game.

However, not all of squash's illustrious names are featured in *Trading Secrets*. Unfortunately, I couldn't entice Heather McKay or Susan Devoy, two greats of the women's game, to share their triumphs – which match would Heather have chosen in a 19-year unbeaten run anyway? – while time ran out on getting hold of a poorly Jansher Khan in Pakistan and Amr Shabana, Egypt's four-time world champion. There is, though, a chapter dedicated to McKay's unrivalled career.

However, one of the aims of the book was to give a flavour of the sport over the last few decades, not just to chart all the top players. I am grateful to those who did commit.

A morning at Azam Khan's house in Ealing was an experience. At the time of my visit, the great Pakistani's own New Grampians Club was being sold off with club membership dwindling. Once he had lamented the sad end to a wonderful chapter, he was away reminiscing on his British Open wins. After my first question Azam then spoke for 40 minutes straight and clearly revelled in recounting the stories.

Hearing from the likes of Chris Dittmar on how he trained in an Adelaide fire station's humidity chamber in a bid to beat the Khans or Rodney Eyles on why he took to unglorified boxing gyms to up his game, were also both illuminating.

And then, just as I was about to submit the book, Egypt's Ramy Ashour won his second world title in Doha, the 2014 final being hailed as perhaps the most remarkable match of all time. Three weeks later, Nicol David, Malaysia's squash queen, won her eighth world title in similar circumstances, the Malaysian saving four match points before overcoming Egyptian Raneem el Weleily in five thrilling games in Cairo. Unfortunately it was too late to make the book, but her 2006 world final win still paved the way to further riches.

I did manage to track Ashour down in New York (it is mystifying but indicative of the sport that the Egyptian, for all his box-office status, largely manages himself) where he was living in an apartment on his own for a three-month training stint. The chapter dedicated to his Qatar crown is made up of several interviews I have conducted with him over the last two years.

Hopefully there will be many more in his presence, if not to spend time with the finest rackets player I have ever seen, including tennis, then to understand what is going on inside the head of this once-in-a-generation Egyptian genius.

He is certainly the most talented I have seen since my first dalliance with squash came as a nine-year-old. I went on to play in my school 1st V and I remember reading reports and looking for results in the newspaper of the top players. Even though I can't recall watching any footage at the time, the names of Eyles, Dittmar and Khan stood out. Nearly 30 years later, those results' recollections were to come to life when their stories were recounted for this book.

Alongside most of the chapters, there are added reflections of the time from *Squash Player Magazine*, the sport's leading publication. I hope you enjoy the musings of these past and present masters of squash as much as I did putting it together. And if you want to understand why the game is so great today, just type in 'Ramy Ashour guitar' on YouTube. You'll have a guaranteed smile by the end of the clip.

Rod Gilmour, January 2015

1

Broken Rackets And Dirty Tricks

AZAM KHAN (Pakistan)
1960 British Open Final, Lansdowne Club
Beat Roshan Khan 9-1, 9-0, 9-0

I WAS just a tennis professional until my brother, Hashim Khan, who died in 2014, won his second World Championship. He came back and said I must take up squash. I only played one game with him when we first played together and I was so tired! It was too much on my legs, but he said I should keep on doing it.

In December 1952, Hashim said he wanted to take me to London. I didn't have any record of note and it was soon the British Championships so I entered into it and won.

In those days, it was a strict entry and only the top 16 could enter. I was denied entry but was given a trial by a Squash Rackets Association official. In those days amateurs were better than British professionals.

I played him and was very nervous, but beat him 3-1 and was drawn against Alan Fairbairne, the British amateur champion who also played cricket for Middlesex. That was what they did back then, they paired me up in the early rounds. I beat him over 70 minutes and met Hashim in the semi-finals. Until then, I had never lost to anybody. So that's how it started for me.

I went to Scotland soon after and twisted my ankle. I was staying at the hotel and asked Jonny Leslie, by then he was a good friend, to take me to hospital and the doctor gave me an injection so I could keep on playing.

The doctor said, 'Don't come back, as it will happen again.' In the semi-final I played Roy Wilson. Two-love up, the leg started hurting and I was now playing on one leg. He took me to five games and Hashim, who was watching from the gallery, told me to come out and quit. But I wanted to finish and the last game felt like an age!

I tried to retrieve one ball from the back of the court and my leg just gave way. Roy had the whole court and he hit the tin! I still couldn't get up and I was lifted out of the court. The next day I had to play the final against Hashim but I couldn't play on. I took the overnight train back to London and the doctors said I had broken my ankle.

The first time I won against him came at the British Open in 1960. Roshan Khan, who was Jahangir Khan's father, was doing the SRA a favour at the time by playing with several top juniors. In return, they changed the rule, the world number one and number two in the same half of the draw. It would mean Roshan would get an easy passage through to the final.

I was playing Hashim in the semi-final and usually, as he was the big brother, I respected him and would never beat him because of that. I didn't want to beat him! I asked him before we went on court whether his leg was holding up. He said it wasn't good, so I said I had better win as Roshan would have beaten him in the final. He agreed to let me win with his permission.

The final at the Lansdowne Club lasted 19 minutes. He got one point in the first game and none in the last two. The spectators had paid £1 per ticket and had made a noise to the SRA as to the quality and length of the final. From that day, the SRA made sure there was a third-place match before the final.

After I won my last British Open in 1962, I went to Canada and won the Open there five times; three times in Toronto and twice in Montreal. In Pakistan, I used to play Hashim and Mohibullah Khan all day. But by now I was coaching in London, having been offered £20 per week. Usually a coach would be offered £6, so I snapped it up.

At the time I was playing lots of exhibitions and in one of them I was playing in long trousers and a sweater. I stepped back to play a forehand shot and I collapsed. I went down on the floor and the Achilles tendon had broken. It felt like someone had stabbed me in the back.

The doctor told me to get to hospital, so I took a taxi to Hammersmith where they told me I would have to have an operation. 'No way!' I said. 'I have to make a championship in Pakistan.' They had sent me an air ticket and an invitation. The prognosis was that it would take several months for it to heal.

One way or another, another doctor friend said I shouldn't go through with the surgery and he would do it. He did it quickly and the leg was in plaster.

At the same time, my 14-year-old son was ill and he was taken to the doctor for tablets. He was getting worse and worse and he told me one night not to go to the squash club to coach. That evening it worsened and we went straight to the hospital. The doctors said there was little chance of survival; I was told there were brain and chest problems.

I took his body back to Peshawar for burial and I was there for two months. I just lost interest with the world after that. Meanwhile, my leg wound was bleeding at this stage and I never had the time to go through physiotherapy to make it stronger.

When I went back to London, I mainly stayed at the club, New Grampians, in Shepherd's Bush. I can't forget him and I still have his photo by my bed.

The following year, the organisers of the Pakistan Championships said that if I could play then I was invited. I still could hardly walk. But a friend who had travelled with me said I should play and it wouldn't matter if I lost in the first round. It would be a chance to see my family and visit my son.

Most of the top players who entered, slept and ate at the club. It was eat, drink, sleep, train for a month. The atmosphere at the club was also very hot! I only had four people supporting me – club members from London who had travelled out also for the championship.

I had to laugh, knowing everyone wanted me to lose. But when you are younger you can do anything, you are strong. So I decided I must win. Why should I lose to these people, even if I was limping? I won through to the final and I was to play Roshan.

It was to be the toughest match of my life. In those days, there was no penalty so the player could do whatever he wanted to stop the other player. If he put his leg in the way to stop me retrieving a ball, the opponent could do this.

I told Roshan not to do any of this though. I said to him that I would have no trouble hitting him with my racket, which I had done before! During one point, he played a drop and I ran forward. When he saw me coming to put the ball away, he put his body in the way.

I also had to contend with cement floors, unlike the wooden floors in England. It was so hot on court. Every point I played I wanted to jump in the swimming pool and this lasted for over two hours and five games.

There was no television recording back then, but everyone who was there said they had witnessed something that would never be seen again.

A few days later I met Roshan again in the Pakistan Open Final. First game, I remember I lost 9-0 and one of the Pakistanis said, 'Now you get the lesson!' But Roshan was also up to his dirty tricks by sticking his leg out and preventing me from reaching the ball.

As I've said, I had hit him before with my racket and was close to doing it again. Again, I laughed to myself. I won the next game before he won the third. The concrete floors were now killing me and my shoes too. I went through three pairs in ten days of squash as I dragged my feet on the floor. I was in pain and bleeding too.

I managed to win again in five games over two hours. I broke a racket as well in the final as I eventually lost patience and hit his leg in trying to make my shot. He was very keen to get his revenge and he was very good then.

But my aim was to keep the ball alive and keep the ball away from him as much as possible. I knew that if I made him work I was going to win. That's the idea of this game after all; you mustn't hit the ball back to your opponent.

Against Roshan, all I was trying to do was to keep him out of position and then hit the front wall and the nick. These days, I rarely see players hitting that nick, it's all up and down, but the Egyptians like to do it.

We never used to let the ball go to the back wall and we caught the ball in the middle of the court. You might not be able to retrieve if you let it go to the back – and if you did you would probably lose the return and your opponent would put it away.

At that time of my career, you only won £50 to win the World Championship. My last British Open win had come in 1962, before the Egyptian Abou Taleb said in the press that if anyone was able to get a game off him he would give them £500. Some of the top squash officials were very upset about this challenge.

Peter Chalk, who was then the vice president of the SRA, was a good friend and living nearby to New Grampians. He said, 'Look, you must play him.' I told

Peter I had lost interest in the sport after losing my son. But he was adamant I could beat Taleb 'with his big mouth'.

Well, I accepted the challenge to play an exhibition challenge match at the Grampians, which was announced in the *Times* newspaper. For some reason, Taleb got edgy and backed out and reasoned that if he lost and returned to Egypt they would 'cut my head off back home' and he would have to live in another country. He knew he was going to lose but he just wanted £1,000 in his pocket before he played.

Anyway, the members at my club – one of them was a top divorce barrister – decided they wanted to bring in a young player called Jonah Barrington and for me to train him. In those days, the court timings were 45 minutes and Jonah could only stay on court for 20 minutes. He was a very bad sportsman then, always crying! I said to him, 'You want to be champion, you stay on court for 45 minutes. If you don't then you're free to go.'

He was doing milk rounds at the time and Jonah soon kept staying and playing. The British Open was looming and he was keen, so after every milk round he would come to the club. In the build-up, I played him and beat him 9-0, 9-0, 9-0 and he was upset by this in the changing room. He refused to play in the championship, but I told him to keep running and playing the ball away from his opponent and he would win the title.

I persuaded him to play and he won the first of his many British Open titles, in 1967. I was still not interested in playing and by now all the top players were coming to visit and I began to do more lessons. It suited me.

How I Got Fit...

I tell you the truth here: myself and Hashim did no exercise. We used to play the British Open and go back to Pakistan in April and play tennis throughout the summer. When Hashim first came over and won the British Open in the early 1950s, a reporter asked him how he was so fit. He said he did 1,000 press-ups and people started copying him. But he wasn't doing anything, but they still reported it! The only exercise we did was on court, by playing yourself. All the people we met were doing gym work and exercise, but I can tell you we did no such routines.

2
Small Town Girl

The story of Heather McKay

IT TAKES just a cursory glance on the web to configure the longest unbeaten runs in sport. Jahangir Khan's 555 matches over five years is considered the best of all, even if the figure is somewhat shrouded in mystery and has yet to be properly verified. There's Olympic hurdler Ed Moses, who between 1977 and 1987 never lost a single race, winning 122 straight.

Then, more recently, comes Esther Vergeer, the Dutch tennis wheelchair trailblazer, who retired in 2013, aged 31, after banking a streak of 470 matches over a ten-year stretch.

There is one record, though, that far outstretches these indefatigable feats. A record that, bizarrely, is essentially a little-known fact, yet stands tall above all others.

Imagine that you take up squash aged 18 when courts are first built in your town, that you compete keenly with your friends and that one day you decide to enter a tournament. Imagine that you win both the junior and senior titles and are encouraged to go on.

You enter the championship of your country, have to qualify as a complete unknown and with only three squash lessons under your belt, having only been playing for one year, you knock out the number one seed and go on to win the title. At 21, you win the world's premier title, the British Open, and go on to win it 16 times in a row. One final opponent you beat in 14 minutes and another 9-0, 9-0, 9-0; and through all these years you are undefeated. You are to be trumpeted by *Sports Illustrated*, in 1977, with a record 'unmatched by any woman in any sport'.

A pleasant dream? Impossible? No, it's the true story of one of the greatest sportswomen of all time, if not the greatest sportsperson: Heather McKay.

Born Heather Pamela Blundell on 31 July 1941, she was number eight of a family of six boys and five girls. Her father, Frank, a baker in the town, loved sport. He was one of the best rugby league players that New South Wales had produced and encouraged all his 11 children to play sport.

There were no squash courts in the town of Queanbeyan, seven miles from Canberra, the Australian capital, until 1959. So, aged ten, Heather took up tennis and then hockey, three years later. She was revelatory at both, won prizes, became Queanbeyan junior and senior tennis champion and played hockey for Canberra. It was a happy childhood.

She wrote in her autobiography, 'Having brothers helped. I was a bit of a tomboy; I kicked a football to my brothers and bowled to them in cricket. That helped my movement and co-ordination when I took up squash.'

On leaving school, Heather took a job in the local newsagent's. She continued to play tennis and hockey, which was how she got started in squash. 'When the courts came, I was a member of the hockey team and several of the girls took up squash to get fit,' she recalled.

Soon McKay had overtaken the other girls and was looking to the men for competition. When the next season came she entered the New South Wales county squash competition in Woollongong and won the junior and women's events.

The following month she was encouraged to enter the important state championships and, being a shy girl, she travelled up to Sydney with her mother and grandmother.

'I won the juniors and had the number one seed two games to one and 9-2 down in the women's and I lost. Was I disappointed? Not at all. I thought I'd done rather well! I wasn't worried because I had just won the junior match and didn't expect to win anyway.'

That performance meant that McKay was picked for the state team to play at fourth string in the Australian Inter-state series, at which she decided that she would also enter the Australian Individual Championships.

'I played in the elimination rounds, got into the draw and then went on to win it. I knocked out the number one seed 10-9 in the fifth. It was close. I beat the No.8 seed in four and won the final in the fourth. That surprised everybody.'

It was a sensational run. An unranked outsider, having played squash for just one year, had become Australian champion.

Disappointment – a rare word in the career of McKay – did follow. Although national champion, McKay was not selected for the Australian team sent to tour Britain. Later she was to admit that, despite her initial discouragement, the extra 12 months gave her more time to hone her game. The decision proved beneficial.

McKay moved to Sydney and worked at the Bellevue Hill Squash Club, and it was during her years here that she met her future husband, Brian. In those days, squash was still an amateur game, and McKay needed to earn her keep and to save for the trip to Britain that was to turn the squash world on its head.

From that first Australian title in 1961, McKay kept winning, with only one hiccup. On her first trip overseas she lost in the final of the 1962 Scottish Championships to the British Open champion, Fran Marshall.

A month later McKay avenged that defeat, winning the British Open Final 3-0 and was never to lose a competitive match again.

'She went into the changing rooms and said out loud that that was the last time anyone was going to beat her, and it was,' Marshall told Squashsite in 2008. 'She always thrashed me after that, and everyone else too.

'She was the best ever player, by a long way. Even in this day and age she would win. I saw a few matches at the [2008] World Open in Manchester and they weren't a patch on her.'

Over the next three years as Miss Blundell and then as Mrs McKay, she won an astonishing 16 successive British Open titles. In that period of total domination she dropped just two games at the Open – that's games, not matches. One was to Anna Craven-Smith in 1964 and one to Sue Cogswell on her final appearance in 1977, at the age of 36.

As well as dominating the British Open, she reigned supreme in Australian events until she turned professional in January 1974. The story of her swift rise to the top and of her long reign as the Queen of Squash would be almost unbelievable if it were not for the records which back it up.

'I played every year in the New South Wales, the Victorian and the Australian. I entered the British and one or two warm-up tournaments in England. Those were the major events I played every year. I held the NSW and the Victorian titles from 1961 through to 1973, the Australian from 1960 to 1973 and the British from 1962 to 1977. I just played these, the odd smaller tournament and league matches.'

Strange nowadays that the world's leading player would play league matches every week with friends.

On reaching the top, McKay kept on improving. Doyen of squash writers, the *Times's* Rex Bellamy, wrote, 'Her capacity for learning was to some extent inborn. But it was developed by remarkable concentration.

'Other natural talents were her athleticism and agility [she was 5ft 6in tall and usually weighed about 9st 4lb], her flair for striking a moving ball, and her superb competitive temperament.

31

'She knew where the ball was going and she was fast enough to get there with time to spare for a balanced, controlled return. Later, she acquired more shots, more variety and the experience to exploit to the full everything she had learned. The outstanding qualities of her game were still persistent power and precision,' Bellamy continued.

The power she generated was simply too much for her opponents thanks to her game being honed and sweetened on warmer courts in Australia.

Being so far ahead of the other women was not a handicap for McKay because she always had men to compete with, and she picked her partners carefully to provide sensible practice and serious competition.

'My biggest asset was my driving. I drove hard and to a good length, probably a little bit better than most girls. My movement around the court was another asset; people told me I was a good mover. There was also the fact that I trained bloody hard, so I knew that if I was getting tired the other girl had got to be feeling worse than I was. Basically, I made them do more work.'

As well as mastering squash, McKay, still shy and horrified at the prospect of meeting strangers and making speeches, fought to combat her self-consciousness and in the end made herself available for interviews and broadcasts.

'Behind her small remaining shield of small-town shyness, she seems forever ready to accept friends and strangers on whatever terms they offer,' said Jack Batten, author of McKay's *Book of Squash*. 'Heather has no notions of showing the world anything except honesty and a smile, and she trusts the world to respond in kind.'

Moving from Sydney, McKay and her husband ran squash clubs in Brisbane and Canberra and in June 1975, moved on to Toronto. McKay, the amateur, managed and Brian, the pro, taught.

After her retirement in 1977, McKay took up racketball for a time to gain the financial rewards that had not been available to her at squash and that few would begrudge her. Within a year, she was the best player in Canada. Later she was to coach squash at the Australian Institute of Sport in Brisbane, training the next generation of young Australian professionals.

Her record stands unrivalled in modern sport. In addition to her 16 British Open titles she won the first World Individual Championship in 1976, conceding just 15 points in the process, and, even though she had ceased to compete in the British Open, she returned to England in 1979, just two years short of her 40th birthday, to retain her world title in Sheffield.

She may have been short of tournament play, but she dropped only one game in the final against home favourite Sue Cogswell. Some feat.

Of all the accolades, one wonders which honours she cherished most. 'There was the first time I won the Australian Open, as an outsider coming from nothing to win it. Another was when I won the Australian ABC Sportsman of the Year Award in 1967. The third was when I was awarded the MBE in the 1969 New Year's Honours list. These are the three things I would choose.'

And all achieved in that 19-year unbeaten run, until her retirement in 1981. Which makes her invisibility, when talking about unbeaten stretches, all the more bizarre. Perhaps it was down to the era. For she played out her career in the amateur days and just before the advent of the women's squash association.

Back then the international fields were relatively small. The old Commonwealth countries took up most of the draws, while the USA was focused on the hardball game. Moreover, McKay's travels to the UK and subsequent thrashings of every English player, most of whom were not full-time professionals, didn't really transcend with the press.

Squash's exposure in the media only took off with the rise of Jonah Barrington, who rubber-stamped the sport with the first signs of professionalism. Barrington got the publicity due to a rivalry, which was certainly lacking in McKay's career.

Perhaps it is best summed up by a colleague, who recalled a changing room debate on the best women's player in the sport. 'Sarah Fitz-Gerald must be the greatest of all time,' he was told.

3

The First Of Squash's Grudge Rivalries

DICKY RUTNAGUR, one of the big hitters in squash journalism for magazines and newspapers for nearly 50 years until his death in 2013, analysed the Benson and Hedges British Open at Abbeydale, forecasting the most dramatic of showdowns, a final between Hunt, whom the Australians claim is the world number one, and Barrington, whom the British say is the authentic world champion. Abbeydale would tell…

Hunt: now with added aggression

Geoff Hunt's last year has seen him, in effect, come to full bloom. His third World Championship; the start of his pro career; and his MBE in the Honours list.

'In that last year alone,' Geoff has said, 'my squash ability and feeling of inner strength and toughness have noticeably increased.' This claim, coming from a person who is realistic yet modest, must be one of the highest significance in assessing his chances of winning back the British Open title, which he won in 1969.

Barring accidents and the most dramatic reversals of known form, the championship should culminate in a final against his old rival Barrington.

Since they established themselves as the two foremost players in the world, Barrington and Hunt have met five times in tournaments. Barrington has won four of these encounters, the exception being the final of the individual event of the 1969 World Championships.

Two seasons ago, they also played a series of 15 matches in more relaxed circumstances. These contests were not advertised as exhibitions, but there was no doubt that the prime consideration was the entertainment of the spectators.

Jonah could not adopt – in fact, he would not have been able to make the effort two or three times a week – to adopt such tactics that have brought him his wins in tournament play. The series ended in a heavy win for the Australian.

There are many facets to Hunt's squash, but lightning speed and explosive power are its essence. When confronted by a 'stayer', he turns on his power in bursts. In four of their five tournament encounters, Barrington has managed to withstand these assaults, but only just.

Reports from Australia, substantiated by eyewitness accounts from South Africa, where Hunt and

Ken Hiscoe were on tour a few weeks ago, indicate that these outbursts of aggression have been more frequent and more sustained. It is also believed that Geoff's opponents can expect fewer errors from him than before.

It would seem that the age of 24 has brought Hunt's squash to its height, and the price on his recovering the most coveted title in the world can be no longer than evens.

Barrington: one question mark over him

And then there is Jonah, four times winner in the last five years, and this time on a hat-trick. Until as late as Christmas week a question mark hung over his appearance. He was suffering from residual toxaemia as a result of impacted wisdom teeth.

Being a perfectionist, Jonah never feels he is fit enough. But when last seen in London, at the final of the Amateur, he seemed genuinely dispirited by the weakness and listlessness left behind by his illness.

The ultimate cure, a dental operation, would have kept him away from the court and training for longer than Jonah could afford at that crucial stage of his preparation. So he had to make do with containment of the infection with antibiotics and pain-killers.

Considering altitude training as the only means of regaining his fitness, Jonah flew to Kenya for three weeks after Christmas.

Strange as it may seem, we know less of the current ability of our own main hope than we do of the overseas contenders. Jonah has not been seen on the tournament circuit since last season.

Each season sees Jonah return a different and more complete player. While Hunt, his main rival, will have to contend with the vigorous squash of Hiscoe in the vital late stages, Barrington will be seeking short cuts past Mohammed Yasin, a pretty complete and capable player, and then probably Gogi Alauddin.

Though the field is one of the strongest ever to line up for this great event, one's money can safely be placed on the competition developing into a straight fight between Barrington and Hunt.

And if you do come to see this epic, make sure you pick up a sandwich on the way, for you certainly won't get away early.

JONAH BARRINGTON (Ireland/England)
1972 British Open Final, Abbeydale
Beat Geoff Hunt 0–9, 9–7, 10–8, 6–9, 9–7

Preparing for the British Open in the early 1970s was like a boxer preparing for a fight and keeping your rival at a distance. The build-up would be for an extraordinarily long period and everything I did was geared towards winning it. It was the de facto World Championship at the time and the press made a big deal of it.

The press men would have been equally disappointed if the match-up hadn't taken place either. But luckily it did that day. The build-up had been from such a great distance. The interviews started from three weeks out and there was huge anticipation.

I always knew in the back of mind that it was going to be a straight fight between myself and Geoff Hunt, my Australian rival. One of the big differences between then and now was that the big players didn't play each other very often. It could be six months or longer, unless you were playing in elongated exhibition tours, which Geoff and I used to do.

However careful the top guys are in the modern game they are going to have to match up for a majority of the year. As far as I was concerned, the domestic competition was never going to match until Geoff materialised. I used to play practice matches as if I was playing the British Open. If my partners didn't like that then that was their problem!

I was never interested in the social side of squash. As far as I was concerned, that was always a good thing for me. It was great to *know thy enemy*, but I didn't want him or anyone else to know that much about me. The less they knew the better.

There was huge respect for Geoff and I really actually quite liked him. For he was the fairest player I ever came across. The concept of a double bounce never came into the equation with him. He called a ball down at 7-7 once against Pakistan's Qamar Zaman in the British Open, which then cost him the match. A year later, he said that he would never do it again as Zaman allegedly cheated.

I always had to get myself conditioned to such an extent that I wouldn't be at a disadvantage when we did play. I knew that if I was training, then Geoff was training. It didn't matter if it was Christmas Day or not, it was getting something in the bank that he wasn't getting.

At that time, I was based in Solihull, in the Midlands. Non-specific training consisted of very strong running, different to Geoff as he was a 400m sprint merchant. What I did was distance running, anything up to ten miles. I was totally ignorant of sport science, but as that developed I incorporated gym work and introduced 200m running into my programme.

Meanwhile, squash was a huge sport developing in Australia at that time. In Victoria, Geoff would have had decent players to spar against and what he tended to do was fulfil his running programme, and then play two or three players one after the other.

It was only later on that he adapted the way he played or became more flexible in what he did. He was robotic and was all about power and precision. He rarely had a bad match and he never did against me, that's for sure.

He developed height and speed and I think the one thing he realised playing me was that I was never going to give him concentrated pace. I would force him to make his own pace, which was more draining.

He would hurt himself as he had a cramping problem. This much was highlighted at the Australian Open once against me when he virtually had to play on one leg due to cramp, while being unable to bring his racket head up fully as he also had cramp in his wrist and arm. Another time in Newcastle, New South Wales, I had to help him out of the court as there was a step in the way and he couldn't get up the bloody thing! He was simply indomitable.

The technique he had was quite exaggerated too but the remarkable thing about Hunt was the way he changed his game in his late 20s when it had been drilled into him how to play the game. He had to step up his game when this young and remarkable Pakistani, Jahangir Khan, came on to the scene. Geoff simply went to the limits and beyond.

Pakistani Gogi Alauddin, who had a masked lob-drop game which was like a bit like a spider's web, always used to pose a problem for Geoff due to his subtle skills, even though he eventually got through in the end.

So, there was only one way to beat him: to keep him on court for a two-hour plus period. Regardless of the circumstances in a match, breaking him down was unbelievably difficult.

In 1972, he was at his most robotic. He was 9-0 and 2-0 up in our British Open Final and I hadn't won a single point in 30 minutes. I can't remember ever being beaten 9-0 in a game before. It wasn't like I was being blitzed over in ten minutes like Ramy Ashour would do today with a succession of unstoppable winners. With Geoff it was a remorseless job in murderous length, a deadly accurate working boast and a simple short game.

It was also error-free and he didn't make one unforced error in those early throes in the final. I told myself to 'keep playing, keep disciplined, don't panic' and an error would surely come. One duly did, then came another.

The context of the match then started to change as his mental rhythm had been broken and he had something else to think about. He would power drives to the back of the court and had great reflexes in the middle. Certainly Geoff would have been an interesting opponent in today's modern era. Most of the top players now stand as close as they can to the short line and get on to the ball as fast as they can. Geoff did this naturally.

The second was crucial. I had to get that game and I was able to get my teeth into it. It then became a full-on battle and the way we both wanted to play. The quicker the ball came on to his racket, the happier he was.

The Yorkshire atmosphere courtside at Abbeydale that day was like a bear pit. The gallery came right down to almost the red line on the back wall. It was remarkably different to the traditional court where there was a huge amount of wall space and the gallery above that.

At Abbeydale, the gallery was all the way around and they were literally hanging from the rafters. It was my favourite court without a doubt. So I was equally disappointed when they changed it and they then asked me to open the new one and I had to tell everyone I thought it was great!

People also couldn't see the whole court, which was a problem when Geoff and I played, with the Australian hitting monumental length the whole time and my coach telling me not to go short from behind!

At 2-1 up, I started to have an attack on court, one that essentially saw my heart go out of rhythm. It wasn't the first time it happened. I had it in the Australian Open first round against Doug Stephenson, probably the nicest Australian ever to go on to a squash court as he was genuinely quite worried about me! Fortunately it settled down, but while it was happening it was difficult to breathe, with the pulse rate going up and up.

So trying to play squash against Geoff under those circumstances was impossible. Geoff sensed I was in trouble and took the game 9-6. He took control of the situation, which was desperate for me.

My pulse rate was flying around so much – a chap in Birmingham once said I had been monitored at over 200 beats per minute when I had previously had it – I couldn't play proper rallies in the fifth and I was down something like 7-2. And then the heart problem suddenly cleared. It was like I was handed a fresh batch of oxygen.

I went up about five gears, which stunned Hunt, as I forced my way back into the match and eventually won. When I came off the court, Nazir Khan, my coach merely remarked to me, 'You were sooo slow on the court!'

◊ ◊ ◊

Eyewitness: How *Squash Player Magazine* reported the final

A deep reservoir of energy, a highly sophisticated sense of tactics and an indomitable spirit saw Jonah Barrington through another cruel marathon with his old rival, Geoff Hunt. The final margin was slight. Battle raged for 115 minutes.

Barrington has now won the British Open often enough to earn him honorary membership of the Khan clan. It was his third triumph in a row and his fifth in six years. Only Hashim Khan's name appears more often – seven times – on the roll of honour.

After the last 16 stage of the tournament, the final was the only match of which the outcome was in the balance. Its dramatic impact was augmented by the weight of the winner's purse (£500) and, even more, by the atmosphere of the new championship court at the Abbeydale.

The glass back wall and the low standing galleries on the side gave the spectators a closer and improved view of the proceedings. They were as close to realising the players' elation, their disappointments and their fatigue as possible.

As the two tracksuited figures of Barrington and Hunt came through the wings at the side of the court, laid down their burden of spare rackets, extra shirts and jumbo-sized towels near the sightboards and then gingerly unlatched the glass door to take the court, the crowd experienced the thrill of being present at a truly big and important sporting event.

Barrington, with the good grace of the perfect host, held the door open for Hunt to stride in first. As Barrington snapped the latch back, the crowd burst into thunderous applause which drowned the sounds of the first few shots of the knock-up.

The new court epitomised the efficiency of the organisation at Abbeydale. Efficiency can be an impersonal quality but, in this instance, it was blended with the warm conviviality which goes with a weekend tournament. Gastronomic needs were splendidly catered to.

Before we get carried away by memories of juicy tenderness of the fillets de boeuf that emerged night after night from the Abbeydale kitchens and the bouquet of the burgundy which washed it all down, let us turn to the flavour and sumptuousness of the battle royal.

Barrington bases every important and difficult campaign on the strategy of playing a long first game. But on this occasion, he could not stretch the initial engagement beyond 15 minutes and, what is more, had the rare experience of being beaten at love. Rallies were long, but never intensely fierce and Hunt came out of the game fresher than his opponent would have wanted.

Only eight hands were played in this game and Hunt had two runs of four points each. Considering the easy pace, Barrington's error rate was high and his responses to drop shots were also slow. Clearly, he looked gripped by the tension.

Hunt continued to make almost hampered progress until 4-0 in the second game. Once more, these four points had been claimed in one hand. At this stage, service changed hands five times without either player gaining ground. Barrington eventually scraped up his first point from a misaimed backhand volley by Hunt. The forehand drive which gave Jonah his second point was only the second winner he had struck so far, in almost half an hour, the first having been at the fag end of the first game.

There were three lets for the next point and getting restive, Hunt again hit the tin. This made it 3-4 to Barrington, who proceeded to get even with a hefty forehand volley.

A deep shot by Hunt on Barrington's backhand got him his service back and another good length took him to five. Barrington almost duplicated this shot to get in again, only to fail on a forcing backhand volley.

Then there was a rare penalty point given against Hunt. Back in hand, Barrington played a screaming forehand winner along the wall. Detecting a slight relief of pressure, he assumed a more aggressive attitude and got up to 8-5.

Hunt gave Barrington's next service the charge and killed it. Twice Barrington was in hand at 8-6, and both times Hunt gained a reprieve with rousing winners. But when he served for the game a fourth time, at 8-7, Barrington broke down on a backhand drive. The fifth time, also at 8-7, he deprived himself by missing with a backhand drop.

It must be said to Hunt's credit that even when hand out, he attempted the most daring shots. He finally came unstuck against a lovely, lobbed service which he just failed to get back.

The vital second game lasted only a minute under half an hour and the third too was of the same duration, although half as many hands were played.

Barrington started hesitantly and Hunt ruthlessly accumulated a 6-1 lead, which he dissipated quite swiftly. Put out by a backhand volley drop, he hit the tin four times running and then put a lob out of court.

At six-all came the most spectacular rally of the match. Ironically, it was brought to a halt by a let. It took a lot out of both players and led to three blank hands. If Hunt had given way earlier to weariness, it was Barrington's turn now to show signs of fatigue as he twice hit down and conceded a penalty point.

So it was game-all to Hunt, at 8-6. Barrington got desperate. He started to cut off the ball earlier and produced two winning volleys in a row.

The next point was controversial. Barrington hit a parallel backhander which Hunt could not reach. He asked for a let which was turned down. Then he queried the validity of an earlier shot. This second appeal was allowed. And still he entered into a discussion (Hunt's side of it was not audible to the gallery), at the end of which the referee changed his mind and ruled no let.

Hunt lost his cool and petulantly hit the tin twice and gave the game away. In light of Barrington's loss of control in the fourth game, Hunt must now bitterly regret his failure to compose himself.

In the fourth, Barrington repeatedly failed to keep his lobs within bounds. It was self-discipline that kept him going 21 minutes through a game in which he looked more tired than he might have ever done previously.

There were no signs of a revival while Hunt climbed to 6-0. The match looked to be heading for a dreadful anti-climax when Barrington suddenly came to life and beat Hunt with a fierce passing volley. Both pairs of legs were getting heavier and slower. There was a penalty point on each side during three blank hands that followed.

Hunt was only three points from victory, but the nearness of it was not a potent enough tonic to revive him for the final effort. The numbness of fatigue set in and the racket head began to drop as he addressed the ball. If he served again and took one more point, it was because Barrington hit a forcing shot into the tin and then ballooned a lob.

Barrington encountered little resistance as, in breathless silence; he went from 4-7 to 7-all. Hunt just couldn't get in front and Barrington finished off the match with two winning volleys.

4

Beating A Khan And The Cramps At Bromley

GEOFF HUNT
1981 British Open Final, Churchill Theatre, Bromley
Beat Jahangir Khan 9–2, 9–7, 5–9, 9–7

I MAY have been edging towards the end of my career, but I was as fit as I had ever been. I trained really hard for the tournament and I was keen on winning as it would have been my eighth Open title, but it wasn't at the back of my mind that Hashim Khan had won seven.

Because of the occasion, my father had decided to travel over to the UK as well. He hardly ever used to travel so that was nice. At the same time, I wasn't thinking that this would be my last ever tournament. I had no intentions of retiring.

I knew how good Jahangir was coming into the tournament and what a good prospect he was, even for a 17-year-old. At that stage, I was beginning to get on top of the other players and beating them quite regularly. Jahangir was the stumbling block and knew I had to beat him to win the title.

I had lost to him in the build-up tournament but I was still confident. He was better than the other players, even though he was still at that age. I could see his standard and I saw him first play when he won his first World Amateur Championship in Australia.

I think other players underestimated him. His fellow Pakistanis thought it would be a little while yet before he came through – but it was far from that. It was within 18 months!

I decided that I needed to get fit for it and prepared especially for the British. I enjoyed that side of it and relished the challenge. Based in Australia, I trained there and then would come over for the tournament circuit in either the UK or South Africa. Training at home was easy but I didn't really have anyone to play with at my level by then. I did a lot of exercise and solo work by myself in the morning and then set up some matches in the afternoon.

By the time I left, I knew that it would take me a week to get back up to top standard. For the British Open I left three weeks before, which was ideal.

The media were quite rightly looking at Jahangir as the main threat. It was obvious, the guy was good, but it didn't worry me. I don't like being beaten, but I still thought that if I played the right tactics against him in particular I could win. I found out a way to beat him; it may not have been good viewing, but at that stage if you put it in the back corners against him in the early days, he couldn't do anything with it. So I was prepared to be patient and frustrate him.

He tended to drive the ball back and it nullified his brilliance. It's how I played it for the first two games. I didn't really care about how it might have looked at to watch, even it was live on the BBC, but it was the only way.

I didn't really think about how Jahangir was feeling after the third. There was lots of waving around from the coaches in his corner, but all I was worried about was how I was feeling internally.

I used to suffer from cramp years ago – I even lost a British Open in the final because of it – I was physically okay, but my salt and electrolyte balance got upset. What used to happen was that after 85 minutes, I used to cramp in an intense way. I knew then I had about 15 minutes to finish the match off otherwise I was out the door. Against Jonah Barrington, I got to 7-0 in the fifth and the cramps took over and I lost.

I subsequently found a way to get over it and, funnily enough, Jonah helped me to counter it after he had finished playing. I was conscious of it. I was taking the right fluids and salts so I didn't cramp in the two hours 15 minutes, which showed that the method I was using was pretty effective. It was the use of slow release sodium. When you dehydrate, you are losing sodium chloride which you need.

I have spoken to a lot of nutritionists, and they advocate that what I did wasn't quite the way they would have gone about it, but it was effective for me!

I did research when the England footballers went to the Mexico 1970 World Cup and how their bodies recovered. They lost lots of weight so they had to keep their fluids up. They recovered within two days so I decided to use these methods in squash around 1974.

In the end I realised it was the sodium, not the potassium that was making the difference. It was knowing the right quantities and trying to get the right amounts into your body.

I needed it in Bromley. It doesn't look like we were moving at all, but I tell you that it was incredibly hard work. The old filming didn't really justify the game back then.

I was starting to get tired but to keep good length and keep in front of Jahangir I still had to volley a lot and look for the ball. It was inevitable that I was going to start to get tired and he got me at the end of the rallies. I knew I was in a little bit of trouble.

It's funny how the match went. I got really tired and I was down in the fourth and feeling pretty average, even though we must have been going for two hours.

Then, I did something I had never done on a squash court before. I was so tired that I decided to relax my body so much that I could conserve as much energy as possible. I knew psychologically that if it went to a fifth game and he was thinking he could beat me, then that would be it. So I had to make him realise I wasn't finished yet. I relaxed for three or four points. I hit the ball tight, hit it a little bit slower and tried not to give him much to play off.

I physically relaxed and let my body go. When I started doing it, my father later thought that just by looking at Jahangir and his coach that they thought they had me. I wasn't trying to pretend, that wasn't my motive.

After I had recovered, I started to up the pace and win a few points back, knowing that the fifth would be a battle. The extra pace made it harder for him, a tactic I hadn't used before in the match. If I could then get on top, I would edge the mental side of the match.

I suddenly found he wasn't reaching the balls like before. I knew I could then win the game. I thought, 'S***, I win this then I don't have to go to five now!'

I tried to not focus on Jahangir too much. I tended not to do that anyway, as they fox you and try all sorts of tricks. Because you are often internally focused and hurting yourself, you probably don't realise what the opponent is showing. That was the case when he rocked back at one point. I barely noticed.

It was a pretty dramatic game in a sense. The subtleties and what was going on was probably not apparent in the gallery, but I can remember it vividly. There were a few errors in the fourth, but in my mind there was no doubt I was going to win, as long as I kept on doing what I was doing.

When you are playing, you don't realise about specific types of shot. Maybe I was opening up the face a little bit more, but that was only to keep the ball up and the rally going. All I was thinking of doing was making sure the pace was up.

I used to play against Gogi Alauddin, he had incredible control and touch, but it was hard for him to combine the pace with it. You could always keep within the game, whereas Jahangir's pace was brilliant. You had to move harder as the ball was going quicker.

I did notice that I had a bit of support in the crowd that day. When I reflect on it, normally people are going to back the younger guy against the current champion. It is a general feeling, but I felt they were supportive of me. Perhaps it was hard on Jahangir, and perhaps subconsciously it had an effect on me.

I had a bit more elation than normal, but I had achieved in what I set out to do. If I had lost I wouldn't have slept all night and would have gone over and over what I did wrong.

In this case, winning the record meant a lot, even though these were my expectations. The emotion was high, especially with my father being there. He was English, born in Kent, went through World War Two. He was a hard task-master, uncompromising, never complimented myself or my brother about our squash.

I knew he would say nice things behind us, but that was our dad. So I was trying to win for our family and my father was the driving force behind my career.

Yet, this was the worst I had ever felt after a game of squash. If matches go to around 90 minutes, my stomach gets churned up and I can't eat because of dehydration. It was a regular occurrence.

But this was more severe than anything. My manager, David Wynne-Jones, and my now ex-wife decided we should go out to a nightclub, though this was the last thing I wanted to do. It felt like I should have been on a drip.

I couldn't drink any champagne and at one point I went to the bathroom and peed blood. I subsequently had some tests done to see if everything was normal. A British Open champion and everyone having a good time bar me.

I couldn't actually eat for the whole week afterwards, my body just couldn't take it. And I was on holiday in Crete then as well. It's funny how the body works: you can still push yourself and it can ignore the other signs.

I got a lot of accolades on the back of the success, whether it was from the Prime Minister back home or not I don't know. Even though I was a professional sportsman I never went out to seek a headline. Because I wasn't controversial enough, I was probably boring in most peoples' eyes. That was just me. I played the sport to win.

The reason I started to get fit was because Barrington came on to the scene. Even then I wasn't doing the right physical work and I paid the price with hip problems.

After Jonah retired we were pretty much at loggerheads. It was hard to get close. When we both finished, the barriers came down and there was a lot of mutual respect for what we did. We became friends in a sense but he's still that elusive character.

I used to enjoy his company and hear him speak. He always has something interesting to say, but we just don't see each other enough.

Sometimes players come through like Ramy Ashour with such a talent, they play who they like and doesn't really see it as a profession. I was the same: I never trained professionally until I was 24 years old, after I had won the British Open and the World Amateur Championships. You can go a long way without necessarily doing it the right way.

◊ ◊ ◊

Dicky Rutnagur knew the ins and outs of 'big time competitive squash as well as anyone', as *Squash Player* first put it back in 1972. After a frenetic British Open Final against Geoff Hunt, Rutnagur profiled Pakistan's new kid on the block, asking whether he could become the greatest player of all time:

There are few instances in sport of sons emulating famous fathers and one of them is Jahangir Khan, the youngest son of the winner of the 1956 British Open, Roshan Khan, of Pakistan.

Still only 17, Jahangir is yet to wear that famous mantle, but he has already taken long strides towards achieving true greatness in his game. At only 15, Jahangir won the World Amateur Individual Championship.

There was no place for Jahangir that year in the Pakistan squad for the team event. But so meteoric has been his rise since then that he played at No.1 for his country – ahead of Qamar Zaman and Mohibullah Khan in the recent championship in Sweden.

Early this year, Jahangir won the inaugural British Under-23 Championship – the successor to the British Amateur Championship – without losing even a single game.

In April, Jahangir became by far the youngest finalist ever in the Audi British Open and was within a whisker of winning it when leading 6-1 in the fourth game of one of the most tense and gruelling finals of all time, against the redoubtable Geoff Hunt.

Considering that Hunt was 2-1 ahead in games at the time. Jahangir may not appear to have been so near winning after all. But not many who saw that epic final would say that Hunt's legs would have coped with a fifth game. All credit is due to Hunt, a man on the doorstep of middle age, to have extricated himself from an apparently hopeless position. But there was little doubt that Jahangir's lack of experience helped open up an escape route for the champion, whom Jahangir had run to a standstill at Chichester, in the tournament preceding.

Hunt, himself hailed as a boy prodigy when he made his first trip to Britain in the early 1960s, said of Jahangir, 'They used to call me the best player ever at my age, but Jahangir is something special, much better than I was at 17.'

Jonah Barrington, himself one of the most worthy and outstanding champions, whose experience and study of the game is deep, predicts that 'Jahangir will become the greatest player of all time'.

The prognosis is based on Jahangir's capacity for hard work, his calm and 'high intelligence'. Barrington believes that 'Jahangir has successfully married the shop window talents of Pakistani squash with Western training methods'.

With his elder brother, the late Torsam Khan, having done a lot of prospecting in his time, the virtues of Western training methods were brought home to Jahangir early in his life.

Jahangir, 12 years Torsam's junior, was already a very accomplished player in the matter of technique, having inherited his skill from a very gifted father. In four years of first picking up a racket, Jahangir, at 14, became Pakistan's junior champion.

The Pakistanis believe in throwing their promising young players in at the deep end and they promptly despatched Jahangir to London to play in the Drysdale Cup. Twice, in 1978 and 1979, he lost in the final to Australia's Glen Brumby, over three years older.

But watching him from the gallery, Torsam Khan, for many years based in England, was convinced that his brother, who was little more than a baby when Torsam left home, was a squash genius.

5

The Start Of Sport's Unrivalled, Unbeaten Record

JAHANGIR KHAN (Pakistan)
1981 World Championship Final, Toronto
Beat Geoff Hunt 7–9, 9–1, 9–2, 9–2

MY PROFESSIONAL career started when I was 17. I had turned pro the previous year and I had started to progress in many tournaments: I had lost in the quarter-finals of the World Championship, won the Brazil and Pakistan Open and then won the British Under-23 event.

I was entering all sorts of tournaments and getting into shape by beating all the top players. My world ranking wasn't that high, but I remember losing only two tournaments that year, one of them being the British Open Final against Geoff Hunt.

I was still young and not that experienced but I had ambitions and missions, and they were to be at the top level. I concentrated at an early age on making sure that happened.

The final defeat gave me a lot of learning material, yet I feel as though I could have won that final too. Just a week beforehand I played against him in the final at Chichester where we played a very amicable two-hour final over five games, the first we had played together.

The British and World Championships were totally different in terms of pressure, even though they are two of the biggest tournaments.

At that time there were a number of top players still there: Zaman, Mohibulla, Gogi. Playing against Geoff was a different matter. He had been at the top for many years and it was a dream to beat him. He was mentally and physically strong and extremely well-prepared. Every tournament was taken seriously and he was one committed player.

After the British Open defeat, I didn't lose a match leading up to Toronto. I had a great chance to win the World Championships and I didn't want to mess it up. It was important for my family and my country as well.

We had some great players in Pakistan, but no one who had got to the top of the world rankings since they were introduced. It was important for me to take the tournament back to Pakistan but I never ever realised that I could carry on like this unbeaten for another five years.

Yes, I had a lot of pressure that year. My focus was on the World Championships; it was just a dream for my family. A lot of people thought I should have won the British Open, even though I was still 17 and inexperienced. I could see the level I had to reach against the other players, so I put all my efforts into my training ahead of the big matches I was going to face in Toronto.

It was difficult for somebody coming into the game at such a young age with these burdens.

There were a couple of players like me trying to reach the top level and Gamal Awad was one of them. I remember I had a tough draw, which culminated in a five-game semi-final with Gamal. I was also carrying an injury at the time, and although I didn't mention it to anybody I could hardly play an overhead shot.

The new technology which was making its way into the sport meant that the 1981 World Championships was one of the first to use the new portable glass court. I loved the new courts and it gave an incredible atmosphere.

In 1984, the British Open returned to Wembley Conference Centre for a ten-year period after spending one year there in 1980. It had the best set-up and best atmosphere in the world at the time. I remember that tickets used to be exchanged on the black market in those days and 5,000 used to come to the semi-finals and finals. The game was really ramping up and people used to come from all over. I have been to many places all over the world, but nothing used to beat playing at Wembley.

Toronto was a big auditorium too, and even though the sport wasn't that popular yet in Canada, fans also came from across America, as well as travelling from London, to watch the final.

Just like the lead-up to the British Open, I knew Geoff was still strong, but I played against him at the

German Masters in Cologne and managed to beat him.

It was the physical side where I knew I had to perform. I had to break him both physically and mentally but I still couldn't underestimate him.

The first game was always really important for me. In Toronto, it didn't matter that I didn't win that opener; it was more about staying on the court for longer. The plan was working out, even though I lost it 9-7.

What happened at the mid-game interval then changed the outcome of the match for me. The date of the final, 28 November 1981, was exactly the same date, two years previously, when my brother Torsam had died.

When I came to England in 1978 for the British juniors, I used to stay with my brother. We were very close and shared everything. I then asked him if I could stay in Sutton, south London, so that I could study and train with him.

It was a great time for me to improve and gain experience from playing alongside Torsam, who at that time was a professional on the world circuit. I learnt a lot and he taught me how to play the game.

That same year, after spending some time back in Pakistan trying to gain selection for the World Team Championships, I was sent to play the World Amateur Championships in Australia.

Somehow, from playing through the qualifying rounds, I won the tournament. Every day I was playing, Torsam used to call me and tell me how to play each player. The coaching gave me a lot of confidence and his positive thoughts – 'you can do this, easy' – spurred me on.

When I came back to London, he went off to Australia for a tournament. Before leaving, he told me that this would be his last before retiring. He said that he would then concentrate on my game and put all his efforts into making me a world champion.

It was a total shock when, two days later, I found out he had died of a heart attack at the tournament. He was only 27. After that, I never wanted to lift a racket again. It was really hard for me.

I went back to Pakistan and stayed there for a few months. After that time, my parents told me that if I didn't want to play squash again, then do it for Torsam. Do it for him and try to achieve the dream that he wanted for me. I made that promise when my father and my coach went to Torsam's grave.

The promise gave me the motivation for thinking about the dream Torsam had of me winning the World Championships. It gave me the extra strength and when Rahmat, my coach, reminded me that it was the anniversary of his death during that first game interval, I focused on fulfilling it.

I knew I was physically strong so I told myself that no matter how long I had to stay on the court, I have to get this title. I didn't want to regret anything out there and I made sure the pressure and my speed went up several levels in the second game.

Coupled with that, the British Open defeat was the best lesson I ever endured.

My determination and focus was totally different after Bromley and that was the moment that I continued to win all my matches for five years and eight months.

The squash standard and the tournament quality certainly seemed to change in the early 1980s. I'm not saying that it was all down to me, but the environment and the game was going up a level in quality.

During the 1981 season as I was training to become world champion, I travelled to the Khyber Pass area for one month. It was high altitude training and at the same time I learnt about my upbringing. Even though I had lived in Karachi all my life, it was where my family was from.

The Pashtun tribe in Pakistan is very famous. Tradition told that they were very brave and hospitable people. It taught me a lot about my background and my father and elders told me many stories, giving me an understanding of who I really was.

It also gave me dedication. I used to do about eight hours a day of training: I got up at around 5am and set upon a ten-mile run at a good pace. If I was in London I would go to the parks, or if I was by the coast I would run on the beach.

I would come back, have breakfast and a rest before going to the local club at around 11am or 12noon where I would spend the next four or five hours. I would play four or five players, one after the other, while I would mix that up with court sprints, gym work and skipping. After the club, I would then spend an hour swimming.

I would do this routine for five days a week and on the sixth day I would play a hard game with any of the top players who were around at the same time.

In those days, the game was all based on fitness, with the scoring system used as hand-in, hand-out. I always believed that if you had strong legs and were mentally fit, you could achieve anything you wanted.

That was the main goal for me; if I was to play at the top level, then I should play all the time like this. That was the reason I always believed that whatever hard work you put in at the beginning, it would always make me motivated throughout my career, until I eventually retired in 1993.

Two or three years after my British Open win, people started to realise it was all about who would come second in tournaments. But to be honest, I never set out to create this kind of record. I wanted to do my best at that time. I never cared about winning or losing the record, for I knew that one day the unbeaten record would come to an end.

Players used to try all sorts of things to try and beat me, but I remember that I didn't even go to a five-game match in five years after losing to Geoff in 1981. I always used to beat my opponents either 3-0 or 3-1.

I played in two different eras. After Geoff retired, the likes of Rodney Martin, Jansher Khan, Chris Dittmar, Ross Norman and Rodney Eyles came along. For 18 months, Ross and I played some great matches before Chris and Rodney took over the challenge. Against players on tour, the matches usually started out with fight, but then they probably realised that they could not get through.

I wasn't a selfish player. Of course, I wanted to win for myself, but at the same time I wanted to help the sport and make it grow. I played lots of exhibitions and played hardball in the United States, where I also won the World Championship there for two years.

Everyone was doing their job and I saw my role as being an ambassador. I was getting paid, of course, but I wanted to give something back to the sport too.

◊ ◊ ◊

Eyewitness: 12 years on, *Squash Player Magazine*'s Ian McKenzie listens to Jahangir Khan's emotional farewell speech in 1993 and reflects on his career

Farewell Jahangir: gone but not forgotten

On a pleasantly warm evening in Karachi, the starlit sky erupted into the cascading colours of the 'ohhs' of the crowd and bangs of the fireworks thundered like the 1812 overture.

One thousand guests sat poolside at the Creek Club for the World Team Championships Opening Ceremony. They strolled on the lawns and feasted at row after row of banqueting tables.

This ceremony, though, was not just a welcome for teams from the 28 countries, but a chance for Pakistan to honour its great players of the past, to show its standing in the world of squash, and for the World Federation to honour its Hall of Fame. But most of all, it was a chance to celebrate the career of Jahangir Khan.

Jahangir was retiring – officially. He had risked a lot that week. No less than humiliation for one of the greatest players the game has ever seen! It was a gamble and a gambler would have got good odds before the World Championship on Jahangir reaching the final.

The gamble paid off, however. With little to gain, except perhaps pride, which had possible been wounded in Johannesburg by pulling out with injury and Cardiff, and national appreciation, he played the final chapter in a storybook career at home. It was his night.

When it came to his turn to speak there was a strong voice that flowed out over the guests – a voice fighting for control, quavering, pausing to clear the tears between the statements.

The honour of all Pakistan was accepted and then thanks given. The dutiful son – son of Roshan, but son also of Pakistan – started with his family and ended with his country.

'Thanks to my great father and my family who helped me throughout my career and for their support,' he said and paused.

Mental images of the quiet, skinny boy who at 15 had beaten England's Philip Kenyon to win the world amateur title, flashed by. Of the young apprentice training at Wembley. Of the miraculous rise to the top as the boy became a man.

Of an epic battle with Geoff Hunt at Bromley that was the end of one era and the beginning of another. Four games, two hours 14 minutes. All the emotions of sport except triumph. First submission, then respect, the comeback, domination, the edge of victory and then defeat.

'Geoff was something special,' says Jahangir when he looks back on that day. 'Even though my brother Torsam is not here today, he has inspired me throughout my career and it's because of him that I am here tonight.'

The death of his adored brother on a squash court in Australia rocked the young Jahangir into months of grief, but it gave him a sense of mission that sustained him in the loneliness of a new country and the long hours of training.

'If it had been left to me, I would not have done it like this. Not for as long or as strong as I did for others. I'm not that type of person. If I take the responsibility, then I do it. Maybe I can't do it for myself, but I can do it for others.'

Cousin Rahmat, experienced on the international circuit, guided the young Khan after Torsam was gone. It was a remarkable partnership and achieved remarkable things. In time, Jahangir would want to assert his own manhood and identity.

It is easy to take for granted now, but imagine the difficulties of his father, Roshan, who arrived in a snowy Britain wearing tennis shoes and a large coat, with just £5 in his pocket. Jahangir had the support that allowed him to succeed so young and he was remembering it.

In the early years there was an innocence and humility, the joy of a Boris Becker winning his first Wimbledon title. This was a champion the press made a legend and were happy to do so. There were deeds that spoke for themselves – the great unbeaten run, the record books rewritten, a defeat that was squash's greatest moment.

There was no need to exaggerate; the themes of sport were there – the rise of a champion, the unbeatable player, the triumph over defeat, the speculation about retirement, humiliation, the comeback and, in Karachi, the triumph again, for one last time.

But to be a legend brings its pressures. 'I would have been ashamed forever if I had not finished it – if I had lost after eight years,' he told *Squash Player* after winning his ninth British Open title to break Hunt's record.

People had heard of Jahangir. What was he like? How did he play? What would it be like to play him? they asked. They came to see for themselves, in their thousands. The game had a star that transcended the sport. Ask someone, ask anyone. Squash? Yes, I've heard of Jahangir Khan they'd say. The growth of the new professional game was the Jahangir era.

Those that went to watch him will remember – the shoulder turning, the body twisting, the catlike spring, the flashing blade, the uncoiling of power in the whiplash action again and again and again until opponents fell.

'Thanks to the players who I played throughout my career and who I will always remember.'

They would remember him, those he played in that great unbeaten run. Matches won: 555. Matches lost: 0. There were players who swore that they were playing a brick wall.

Those he played will remember, too, that he would last longer – two hours 46 minutes it took Gamal Awad to find that out in 1982 – hit harder, get there faster.

There was a pressure you just couldn't live with. Players? Take the British Opens he contested and won and the players he defeated – Hiddy Jahan, Awad, Qamar Zaman, Chris Dittmar, Ross Norman, Jansher Khan twice and Rodney Martin three times.

'I won't be playing in international ranking tournaments again and I will miss the game,' Jahangir said. 'Thanks to Allah that I could finish at the top and in good health. Thanks to the Pakistan Squash Federation.'

No, thank you Jahangir.

6

The Man Who Ended Khan's Run

IN 1985, *Squash Player Magazine* spoke to Ross Norman, the world's number two and a position that the rest of the players would rather do without. With Jahangir so firmly entrenched in the number one position, they would like to think the number two spot available, but in the previous 12 months Norman had not only come back from a disastrous leg injury, he had lifted his own game up several notches and the gap between the two and three spots was as wide as between the one and two spots.

Norman reckoned to have played Jahangir about 20 times – in fact in the previous six months he had played him in five finals: the US Open, the Canadian Open, the Swiss Masters, the World Championship and the World Team Championship. He lost on each occasion but still felt that the world champion could be – and would be – beaten.

How do you feel now when you walk on court with Khan?

I always feel that I'm in with a chance – you have to feel that you have a chance or you will feel disheartened. Building up towards the World Championship I believed I did have that chance and went in there with a positive attitude and I felt I did come close.

Did you have any approaches or game plan?

Not really. I just wanted to make it as long as possible because I feel that the longer you stay on court with him the more chance you've got. The first guy that is ever going to beat Jahangir is going to do it in 150 minutes. It's going to be a long, long hard match.

Isn't that exactly the wrong way to approach Jahangir in view of his awesome fitness and strength?

You've got to work on your fitness and the way I see him being beaten is him having a tough quarter-final and a tough semi-final and if you're prepared to stay on court a couple of hours you've got a chance. It's going to take that combination to beat him.

But the truth is that you are the one who has the tough quarters and semis and Khan's opponents give up.

That's what happened in the World Championships – I didn't exactly have an easy path, the last 16 and quarter-finals and semis were relatively easy 3-0 and I was pretty fresh when I made the final which is why I could do well.

He has the aura of invincibility – does he have any weaknesses?

He has very few weaknesses. I believe he is the best squash player that has ever been. He's got the fitness that Geoff Hunt had. I think he's got even more determination than Hunt and he's more aware that he hits more precise shots. He hits the same shots as Hunt and he cuts them more and so the ball stops that inch closer to the front wall which makes all the difference.

When Davenport took a game off Khan in the British Open, he seemed to be having the most success with the short game – is that one way of decreasing his superiority?

A lot depends on Jahangir. If he's playing well there's just no one who gets a game. But if he's a little bit off and you're on then you have a chance – it has to be that combination. When Davenport takes a game it's a lot through shots but then again it's only a matter of time before he loses. Qamar Zaman has better shots than Davenport and he hasn't taken a game off Jahangir for years. So it's not that kind of game that's going to beat him.

It seems as though the gap between Khan and the rest is widening.

I don't think so. That gap has always been there – it's just that more people are getting discouraged now, that's all. Jahangir, like Hunt, is a true champion and he can raise his game by I-don't-know-how-many-per cent when the occasion demands it. So that when a challenger comes along who is consistently taking a game, he raises the level.

Remember when Hunt was champion and Zaman and Mohibullah came along, he raised the game to consistently beat those guys and when Jahangir came along he raised his game again. That's the trait of a true champion.

You're making him sound even more invincible.

No, there has to be that combination. If he met Gawain Briars in the quarters and then Chris Dittmar in the semis – Chris has come very close to taking two games off him – and say myself in the final – or any combination of those players in any order – he could be beaten. The guy is only human – he does get tired. I don't have nightmares about him. I just have to raise my game and I think I have in the past 12 months, just that my approach to the game has changed. I don't seem to get stale any more. I prepare myself a lot better for the matches. I cut out errors which used to creep into my game.

What advice would you give a young player who is setting his sights on Jahangir?

He'd have to be good for a start. He'd have to be in the top 16 in the world before he started challenging. He would have to go out and get really fit and prepare himself mentally. The person who beats Khan will be the person who out-Jahangirs Jahangir! Be fitter than him, be more accurate than him and be more aware on court than him. Because Khan's game negates everything else. You can have all the flair in the world but Jahangir can negate that, he'll neutralise everything you've got. That's how Khan made it – he out-Hunted Hunt.

◊ ◊ ◊

ROSS NORMAN
1986 World Championship Final, Toulouse
Beat Jahangir Khan 9–5, 9–7, 7–9, 9–1

Here's a fact: Jahangir Khan was going to lose one day. You almost had to live in that moment in the first half of the 1980s to understand how a sportsman could dominate for so long without ever losing. A five-year unbeaten streak was some feat.

Every time I went to a press conference, the media would always ask me when he might be beaten. They would always target me as I was world No.2 and the closest person to him. I said, 'Look, there's two things here: one day he will be beaten, unless he retires unbeaten, and two, I would like to be that person.'

Jahangir had broken several players, in particular Egyptian Gamal Awad. He never beat him and they had some great matches, but in the end he couldn't find a way through. He never really recovered after that.

So for that person to beat Jahangir, they would have to stay on court for up to two hours. So it was in 1986. I could just feel the other players in the pre-World Championship press conference thinking that to stay on court with him for even an hour was perhaps too much.

That was the way you had to do it. By playing your best squash, by being the fittest you had ever been. And for me it all came to a head in that championship.

As in any era of squash, you have to be fit, agile, fast and strong. But with all those qualities, it still doesn't mean that you are set to become a world champion. You need those before you set out. Everything is more refined today, but basically it is the same game.

Perhaps if I didn't have a parachute accident three years previously, I would never have been in that position in the first place.

Before 1983 I had been happy with my progression into the world top ten. I was earning good money, contracts and travelling the world. The accident was a huge wake-up call for me, while the incident was the single biggest thing to help me win the world title: the realisation to do the best I could in the time I had left as a professional.

But at the time it was reckless. When you're 23, you think you are bombproof. My father was a pilot and I used to go up with him and see people jump out of planes. I had always thought at the back of my mind that I would do it one day.

I had money so I just went out one quiet afternoon in the off-season down to Thruxton, near Andover. What was the worst that could happen? Well, I landed and damaged my knee pretty badly.

If I hadn't gone parachuting, would I have won the world title? I doubt it. But when I returned to the tour a year later, I focused my game around beating Jahangir. I figured that if you did that, then you could beat most people.

I tried to apply as much pressure as I could in the rallies and volley when I could. If I was working the opponent, then there was a good chance I would overcome him as I was fitter and lighter. Movement is a massive deal in squash and Jahangir had that in abundance, as well as shot-making and sublime stroke play.

My game had nothing special about it. I tried to do everything about it to the best of my abilities. I had no real weak points and when I saw Jahangir go to the top of the game, I followed him. There was no science or technicalities behind it.

People say that Jahangir had only played around seven tournaments that year, but he won the lead-up event, the Canadian Open, in true Jahangir fashion. He thumped everybody and certainly wasn't out of practice by the time it came to the worlds.

I had a massive semi-final against Australian Chris Robertson, which went to around 100 minutes over four games. It didn't do me any favours to play Jahangir the next day. I remember saying to my brother that I surely couldn't last the pace. Even if I got just one game off him, it would feel like a victory.

I just didn't feel like this would be my day. Other times I would have put my house on winning, but not then. You can train hard all you want, but you can't train for a semi-final and final of those lengths, especially a semi-final in the evening and then the final, which started the following afternoon.

The crowd attendances were tremendous. There were around 3,000 people there and the French crowd were truly fantastic. They were behind me, but they had still come along to see Jahangir win yet another World Championship. They went to see the world champion in action, not the result. I was the underdog and I felt like they wanted an upset to happen.

There was no one there to sit with me to talk about the game. There were perhaps only a few players who did have a full-time coach at that time, Jahangir included. I had my younger brother in my corner during the world final. He was a coach at Fontainebleau in the Loire Valley. It wasn't technical coaching in any way; I had always preferred to do things on my own.

Yes, I held it together against Jahangir longer than I had at any time previously against him. But the trouble was that I had played against him 30 times previously, and 20 of those had been in major finals all around the world, the New Zealand, Spanish, European and World Opens.

The match took a while to settle down. It was like a rugby game where it takes a few rucks to get into the groove. I was tense and anxious, but having played in the world final the previous year and got a game, it gave me the confidence for future assaults.

And I got the first game – a part of the game that Jahangir himself said was always the most critical. You start to reassess the match. I then won the second. That meant Jahangir would be taken to five, which hadn't happened since 1981. Everything started to feel good.

At two-love up, it was a shock. But it would have been headlines if I had lost in five and the fact he had been taken to a decider.

It was a high-paced game and great quality squash and as the points ticked by, there was a niggling feeling that he hadn't been tested like this for years. Added to that, I was feeling good, really good.

He used to pump the length – which he was awesome at – wait for you to defend and then go and hit the winner or intercept. In the final, I was matching him. If he hit a loose one, I would win the point and give him the run around.

After he won the third, I had him at 5-0 and 8-1 in the fourth. I was totally in the zone. I was blocking it out and by now it was point by point. Even when I got to eight, I told myself that I was at seven. I could say that to myself in the heat of the moment – and believe it too. Many a sportsman has choked at that stage and funnier things have happened, but I simply didn't want that person to be me.

I won the world title on a cross-court drive. He took me up to the front and I think he thought that I was going to put in a drop shot, but I heard him start to come forward and smacked it across the court. It died in the nick on the side at the back. A lucky shot, but I took that!

The crowd went nuts and my first thoughts were that I had achieved what I set out to do. It didn't matter what I did now in the sport. It certainly changed everything, more so that up until then there had only been two world champions, Geoff Hunt and Jahangir.

There had been some mutterings about a 'wobbly' ball during the match. It depends who you talked to. If you talked to Rahmat Khan, Jahangir's coach, he was just looking for an excuse. The ball had been used before in other tournaments. It was a Merco design, and had reflective strips on the outside. What it did was that if you shone a light down, it would reflect off the ball so television could pick it up. It wasn't so much wobbly, than skiddy.

Occasionally it did skid, but on that day I don't think it did it once in the final. There were no complaints and not even Jahangir complained during the tournament. I think because he had lost and critics were trying to reason as to why, there must have been something else factored in. I'm not being cynical about it – and the Dunlop ball was perhaps better – but he was absolutely ripping the ball. No one got near him until the semi-final where Chris Dittmar, the Australian, got a game off him.

Where it was good was when it got me out of trouble. I could use a high skid boast, which is when you're deep in the corner and you don't want to boast out, but you can't drive it, you aim upwards, so it skids off the sidewall, high on the front wall and goes back on the other side. That was very effective for me.

Such had been the general feeling before the final, that one of the media later told me that they had already written the story. The deadline to get it in on the Tuesday was something like 7pm. The rumour goes that they had already written the story and all they had to do was fill in the result. So, there was a hasty retreat after having to do this for the first time in over five years. I thought that was hilarious.

I don't have a problem with it, but 90 per cent of the articles were about Jahangir losing, rather than that there was a new world champion. We turned professional at the same time in January 1980 and I witnessed him going streets ahead. There were seven or eight guys ahead of me and one-by-one I ended up at number two and trying to challenge him.

The game had opened up in May 1980. Up until then there was a division between professionals and amateurs. Like Wimbledon had been, you couldn't play if you were pro and you had to be an amateur. Squash was very much like that.

I was more focused on becoming world champion than beating Jahangir. The question is what would you rather do: beat Jahangir in a tournament other than the World Championship, or win the world title without him in it? The answer is obvious: winning the World Championship.

If ever I was going to win the worlds it was always going to be around 1985 or 1986. Who knows if I was ever going to win another big title? And sure enough I didn't reach the next year's final as Jansher Khan reached the final and had announced himself on the scene.

You can understand why the publicity would go with Jahangir. You just assumed it. You accepted it. I wasn't craving it and it was just a personal thing. At least I was world champion for 12 months – and not many people had said that prior to Toulouse.

I got a telegram from the Prime Minister. I won numerous awards, but I couldn't go back and accept them as another big tournament was always round the corner and I had to keep playing. New Zealand later organised three challenge matches against Jahangir in different venues and he beat me in all three. I got close in one of them.

However, what happened immediately after winning in Toulouse was that Jahangir was on 520-

odd points and I was around ten points behind him in the world rankings. The next opponent was streets behind.

The rankings came out a month before the World Championship, which they used to base the seedings on. Before Toulouse, I went off back to New Zealand to play my home Open, which I won. My average points were reduced down, but had I not played it, a tournament would have come off and I would have gone to world number one. So, I played a tournament, won it and it stopped me becoming the world's top player.

Having said that, I wonder how Jahangir would have reacted to me being number one seed for the World Championships. Would I have beaten him still? Who knows.

How I Got Fit...

I used to lob from the back, but with Jahangir he was great at pulling it out of the air and hitting straight into the nick or using the volley drop. I used to lob down the walls or drive if I was in trouble to get the length right, rather than boast. If you did that then it was pretty much over.

The lob isn't used a lot these days, apart from Nick Matthew in the modern era. Certainly I think it is an underrated shot and has been lost over the last decade. You can use it as an attacking shot too. There used to be a great Pakistani player, Gogi Alauddin, who was a master of the lob. He wasn't particularly big, he was skinny and he used to push it around. He wasn't a powerful player, but that shot got him to a British Open Final.

I put a lot of emphasis on training. It used to get me out of a lot of sticky situations. But we really didn't know back then what the right training programmes were. I kept it as close to squash as possible, so I did court routines and sprints and generally put in the hours. There was very little in the gym.

An average day would be 12 sets of one minute to finish off the training session. Sometimes I would do ten or 12 sets of 50 if I was going to a tournament in South Africa, which worked out at around two minutes 20 seconds for each set, touching the top of the tin and sprinting back.

It was a basic routine but it suited me. Today it is a lot more refined and I would have listened to the experts, but this kept me fit. You devise your own programme and run with it.

◊ ◊ ◊

Eyewitness: Martin Bronstein was in Toulouse waiting to write another valedictory report on Jahangir Khan's latest world title. How the tables were turned.

There are times, I am sure, when Lady Luck, Fate and The Gods sit down in the back room of a pub somewhere in Eccles and get legless on cases of Scotch supplied by the Bookies Association. The bookies do this when they want the form books upset, when they need a new Rolls, a world cruise, or enough money to pay for a physics lab at an exclusive school where they wish to enrol a less than bright offspring.

On this occasion, they were all under the table, not just from the single malt but from laughter, having read the prognostications of the British Squash writers who had covered the national newspapers with the fact, based on their deep knowledge of the game, that A Certain Gentleman from Pakistan was an absolute certainty to win the World Championships for a sixth time, just as night follows day, as sure as privatisation follows nationalisation.

Toulouse is a long way from Eccles; we sat waiting for yet another Khan win, 3,000 of us, the television cameras taking the match to possibly millions more.

The Palais des Sports was a modernistic-looking piece of 'floating roof' architecture constructed without interior pillars. It is an arena rather than a sports centre and sat something like 7,000, but for the World Championship it was under half that, the layout limiting seats around the Perspex court.

Unlike the English Perspex and glass courts, the French model has no visible means of support – a characteristic in common with most squash players. There are no iron girders at the corners over the top, the structure relying on the integral strength of the Perspex panels with their flying buttresses. If this sounds a bit shaky, in use it is just that – with the walls vibrating alarmingly when a player made contact. Nevertheless, most of the players said it was the best of all the transparent courts they had played on.

Norman went out on court and did what he always does, plays as tough as he knows how. They battled, the world's two best squash players by a mile, head to head point to point with never more than two points separating them.

Khan seemed to be weak at scraping the ball off the forehand wall by the service box. Norman was hitting the ball crisp and low and forcing Khan into errors. Norman also felt that the referee was making strange decisions, made his customary short, sharp comments and got on with it.

Leading 6-5, Norman hit a beautiful clip boast which caught Khan at the T to get hand in. Then he hit a fierce drive off his backhand which had Khan going the wrong way and was two points away from the game. Khan tried to hit a ball off the backhand wall and saw it hit the tin. Norman stood at game ball and the temperature rose at the prospect of Khan losing a game in two successive matches.

They got involved in a dropping duel at the front of the court with Norman hitting the winner and taking the opener. The French crowd went slightly wild to the amusement of the Knowledgeable Ones in the press box who knew this was just a mere hiccup.

Norman came out breathing fire and took the first point with a rocket cross-court drive. He ended the next rally by driving Khan into the backhand corner and cutting his reply into the nick.

Khan gave him a third point by backhanding the ball into the tin from the centre of the court. It looked as though Norman had finally broken the jinx. The theory had been that if you took the first two games from Khan, he would crack under the unaccustomed pressure.

Then came a series of referee decisions, right or wrong, that gave Khan three strokes in five rallies – and a denial of a let for Norman.

From being 3-2 up, Norman was 3-5 down. He was boiling and came out of the door and asked to speak to the tournament referee. John Robinson, the referee, pointed out to his marker and said, 'Here he is.'

Norman, taken aback for a second, then asked the tournament referee, Patrick Bigeard, if he agreed with all the referee's decisions. There was a long pause before he uttered the word 'yes'. Norman recognised the pause for what it was and said, 'No you don't,' and walked back into the court and asked Khan if he wanted to change the referee.

Khan said, 'It's the same for both of us so why do we change?' The game continued and I fully expected Norman, his concentration and groove ploughed up, to just fold. But Norman has enormous determination and single-mindedness and fought back to five-all when he embroiled with the ref again.

Norman has never been one to lose his cool – at this point he was boiling with rage. But Robinson is the Chief of Police for a London borough and at one point ran the London riot squad and would not be intimidated by a mere squash player. He told him to get on and play squash and when the game was 25 minutes old gave Norman an official warning for wasting time.

Khan was making errors, more errors than he made in any four matches. They were the errors of a tired man. He said afterwards that the ball was skidding and when he went for a winner, it hit the tin and it destroyed his confidence.

Norman was almost error-free. Once more he stood at game point after Khan had twice hit the tin when serving at seven-all. Norman drove to the back,

Norman lunged and hit a back wall boast which hit the front wall and sat up.

Norman lifted his racket high and did a beautiful cut into the tin. He was half an inch away from being 2-0 up. He turned his eyes heavenwards and then closed them, trying to blot out the memory of the last shot. But Lady Luck, Fate and The Gods had made their decision – Khan could not get back into the game and after 41 minutes and 35 seconds, the second game finished with Norman winning it 9-7.

The drunks of Eccles hadn't finished – they needed a little more fun out of things and Khan came out and ran up a 7-4 lead and just when we though the natural order of things was taking off, Norman roared back, hitting a superb slam down the left wall to tie it up at seven-all. Khan persisted and got the next two points to avoid a clean sweep.

Even Norman thought that once Khan had taken the third game, the match would take a turn for the worse.

The fourth game was over in under ten minutes. It was almost anticlimactic, but the French crowd wouldn't allow that sort of *tristesse* to creep in. Khan looked beaten. He failed to attempt to get a Norman drop – the unthinkable had happened – Khan was tired, he'd stopped running.

When Norman stood at 8-1, the mind went numb. When he hit a cross-court drive to Khan's backhand which his lunging racket failed to reach, there was a period of disbelief.

Then bedlam and pandemonium echoed around the world as squash hit the headlines in a way that it surely has never done before. Strange that it wasn't a great victory that made the world telephone Toulouse, but a defeat. This is an enormous tribute to Jahangir Khan. The victory was a just and fitting reward for Norman, the man who never stops trying, who doesn't know how to quit, even after almost destroying his knee in a parachute accident.

Khan, meanwhile, wasn't up to par – his layoff due to a ligament injury in Malaya took a greater toll than he realised. He said he knew he was taking a risk in entering the World Championship, but the title meant a lot to him.

He had played the Canadian Open a week before and had his usual easy trip to the winner's rostrum. Certainly the Merco TV ball is a disaster and did some strange things, but as Khan said about the referee, it was the same for both players.

7

A Burning Desire To Beat The Khans

CHRIS DITTMAR (Australia)
1989 World Championship Final, Kuala Lumpur
Lost to Jansher Khan 7–15, 6–15, 15–4, 15–11, 15–10

GROWING UP in Australia, I would listen to late night radio in my brother's bedroom, when the BBC radio reports would come after midnight on Sunday evenings. I would hear how my fellow Australian Geoff Hunt had got on against Jonah Barrington in the British Open Final. That was how romantic squash was for me.

So to start out playing a group of Pakistanis: Mohibullah 'Mo' Khan, Jansher's older brother, and Gogi Alauddin, I genuinely had to pinch myself. You had never seen anything like it, especially when they hit the ball like you've never seen, at a time when wooden rackets were being used.

As my career blossomed and focus turned to the 1989 World Championships, I still hadn't beaten Jahangir Khan.

I knew a year in advance that the worlds were going to be in the Malaysian capital and I thought to myself that I have to do something different. How on earth was I going to become a world champion if I happened to be playing a Khan in the final there? In any other city I would have gone in with my normal training regime and some kind of confidence in my ability. But oppressive conditions? No chance.

But the short story is that whenever I played in Asia, Singapore, Kuala Lumpur or Hong Kong, the humidity was seriously oppressive and I suffered. During my time on tour, I was also one of the biggest. I was probably twice the size of Jansher and bigger than Jahangir.

So I decided to do something different. I went to my local fire brigade in my home town of Adelaide. Such were the modern ways back then, for 1989 at any rate, that they had a brand new humidity chamber installed, about two-thirds the size of a squash court.

I contacted the fire chief of the station and asked him if I could come into the chamber every day for two months so that I could run up and down, with a few other requests: to bring my stepper and an exercise bike. He gave me the nod and I set about going in for 60 days straight.

I know that the Australian Institute of Sport has one nowadays, but, to my knowledge, this hadn't been done before back in 1989. It meant that when I flew to Kuala Lumpur, I travelled as a different athlete. I was confident in both mind and body. At the end of the day, you have to believe in what you are doing – especially when you are playing in the era of the Khans – and for the first time I really did.

I had flogged myself in the chamber, to the point where a two-hour-plus match was well within my capabilities. Perhaps it was down to a shocking machine called a versa climber, which is a machine akin to climbing a mountain where you are pulling yourself up with your arms and your legs at an incredibly high intensity.

It saved me running on my feet for two hours. It was similar to a stepper and I wasn't pounding the ground. I had put a lot of thought and science into the build-up, seeking the advice of a sports scientist from the South Australian Institute of Sport, Neil Craig, which again was an unusual thing to be doing.

I don't mean to sound egotistical, but the guy I met turned out to be a bit of world-leader in his field. He was terrific and got me fitter than I had ever been before. He had monitored my heart and Neil came to the conclusion that I 'struggled in the heat, struggled in humidity, so what if we trained in this chamber for two months?'

As you would, I immediately said, 'Mate, I'm trying to win a world title. I'll do anything.'

I never actually hit a ball in the chamber, despite the size of it resembling a court. It was all about the physiology and being prepared. I call it a humidity chamber, but really it was climatic. They could set it to any conditions they liked and it probably meant a five-to-15-minute training drill for most of the fire crew.

In the end, my regime drew a crowd. I had Aussie Rules football teams coming to watch me train and all sorts of things happening. The word had got out and most people thought I was mad. I think this was down to Neil, who clearly used me as a guinea pig, given the fact that he was also an AFL coach!

I would go in first thing in the morning and work around the fire brigade's schedule. But they, like most people in my home city, were so supportive and accommodating.

On a scale of one to ten, it was probably a 9.5 in terms of experiencing the worst thing you could possibly do in your life. It wasn't fun, that's for sure. Put it like this: as a big bloke playing in Malaysia for the first time, and say you are two-love down in games in a non-air-conditioned court, you are thinking to yourself, 'What the **** are you doing here!'

You are playing a bloke who is sprinting around, thinking nothing of it. Sure enough, I didn't last too long on day one, but I slowly built it up and I got used to it.

The mental side of the sport really interested me, especially knowing that if you flew into a country where Jansher and Jahangir were unbeatable, then you were already on the back foot. Now, though, I was accustomed to the conditions and a genuine world champion contender as soon as I flew in.

Not many people knew about what I had been doing. It was pretty much a secret outside of Adelaide. In cricket, they call it sledging, but in squash I called it 'getting on the front foot'. I used to tell everyone how hard I worked, how hard I had trained during my career, to the point of being an idiot really.

There was an English player called Del Harris, who ironically went on to work for the fire brigade after he stopped playing. I showed him a bit of disrespect one day and he nearly beat me in Singapore during one tournament.

I went for a coffee with three of his fellow compatriots beforehand, where I let slip, 'Yeah, perhaps I shouldn't have run all those 400m sprints this morning.' It was an absolute lie but I wanted to get inside his head. They were some of the things I did.

Perhaps I should have arrived in Kuala Lumpur and pronounced myself with my best Muhammad Ali impersonation that I'm here and I'm the fittest man too. But I didn't and tried to keep it a secret.

I don't remember anything of the early rounds. All I remember is the semi-final and the final within 24 hours of each other; two of my biggest days on a squash court. To play Jahangir then Jansher back-to-back was bloody hard work and that's all I really recall.

It was a long and hard semi-final against Jahangir. I was maxing for the whole match. There were no lulls or easy periods. It was full-on throughout its entirety and it was the way you had to play against him.

I was generally a very conservative player and never went for anything risky or dangerous. But at 14-14 I did, and for some reason I thought it was 's*** or bust here'.

He served a very high lob serve to my backhand side and I hit it cross court straight into the nick. The whole auditorium erupted. I only had to win two more points but it seemed to stifle him and he didn't chase or try in those subsequent points.

It was just uncharacteristic that I would do something like that at such a crucial time of the match. But it broke him and two points later he shook my hand. I hit a ball on match point and he didn't chase it. I had beaten Jahangir for the first time ever.

Perhaps I should have tried that ten years earlier and who knows how many world titles I might have won! But in regards to this match, it made me actually beat him a lot more times afterwards. I had taught myself to just stay with him. Even when I was vomiting during games, it was a case of just 'keep going, keep going until breaking point'. And lucky for me, there were breaking points.

It was one victory that held me in great stead for the rest of my career, even though I was unable to ever win the world title – and I did play in five finals in all, never to win one.

But to play against Jahangir was a thrill. He was an absolutely brilliant racket player. If you could compare two people, well, Jansher was a marathon man who could run forever. Jahangir struck the ball better than anyone, even by today's modern standards.

Those two days in Malaysia at least taught me that you wouldn't beat the best in the world by hitting a backhand volley into the nick at 14-all. It may win you the odd point here and there, but it would also lose you a lot too. And it would never bring you titles. There was just no substitute for working hard.

I had always been someone to hold respect on court, too. When a player such as Jahangir beats you for ten years and then you suddenly beat him for the first time, I was of the mindset that if you suddenly punched the air and did cartwheels, you owe every opponent to look them in the eye and shake their hand.

I don't want to sound like a wet blanket, but I had prepared in my mind that one day I was going to beat Jahangir and when I do I will show him the respect he deserves. I would be celebrating on the inside and be really happy.

I also genuinely believed that I was there to win the world title and I had one more day to go. So if I didn't look too displeased on winning that final point, it was probably a combination of the two.

The Malaysian people adored Jahangir, but I received equal praise from the fans that day. The *Daily Telegraph* correspondent at the time was Dicky Rutnagur, a ripper of a bloke. He happened to be sitting with my wife, who was crying her eyes out and he gave her a handkerchief. That's what I remember most about coming off court!

I was now super-confident going into the final against Jansher. But my record against him had also been terrible, so when I was leading 2-0 and one game away from the title, perhaps it was inevitable that a seed of doubt started to be sown.

I hit the wall. I started to feel exhausted and started to find any bit of energy to keep me going. He got back and levelled at 2-2 and he was totally outplaying me. It was demoralising to think that I had the better racket skills that day, but he was running rings around me.

You wouldn't believe it, but in the decider I then raced to 9-0. It's here that I will forever take a moment to my grave that I wish I could turn back.

I walked to the front of the court to pick the ball up after it had hit the tin. I was there for a second and said to myself, 'I am going to be world champion.' From that moment on, I barely won another point.

You can't be in any more control than being 9-0 up, with only six points needed for victory. Very quickly he turned it around. He was running like a gazelle, I was stuffed and it was a very harsh, ordinary lesson to learn.

With no disrespect to Jansher, Jahangir was five times the player, but in the end Jansher did end up with a formidable record.

When you were on court with them, it was like playing John McEnroe, who just made the ball talk, serve and volley, and basically do anything he wanted. Or Bjorn Bjorg, who hit seven bells out of the ball until he beat you. That was the analogy of drawing either of them.

Jahangir was just a phenomenal squash player and the best I have seen in my lifetime. The psychological part of sport was set up with that win against Jahangir in the semi-final just a week later, too, when Australia played the World Team Championship final in Singapore.

Jahangir was at number one and Jansher Khan at number two for Pakistan and Rodney Martin and I beat both of them to win the team title, which, as an Australian, was a very sweet and proud moment for me.

It was also a special day for us as an Australian team (team-mate Chris Robertson also won) and we celebrated for many days after that.

Even though I never won the world individual title, at least they knew of my achievement back home. My father rang me soon after and told me a story about how he was at an AFL match and at half-time the MC told the crowd, 'Chris Dittmar has just beaten Jahangir Khan in the world semi-final.' Fifty thousand people applauded and cheered.

I suppose it was a special moment on hearing that. Adelaide was – and is – quite demanding when it comes to sport. Whenever I used to go home, I would get people asking me, 'Chris, when are you going to beat this bloke?' I had been listening to this for ten years. So dad was tickled when he heard the cheer. For me, it was some kind of justification that I had finally done it.

And the humidity chamber? Well, I never did go back in there. It was something to do with a lost key.

◊ ◊ ◊

Eyewitness: How *Squash Player* reported it

Twice before – in 1983 and 1987, Chris Dittmar had fought for the world title and lost. Twice in the 1989 final, that title was within his grasp but ran away from him.

At 13-13 in the fifth, Jahangir served. Before it landed the tall left-handed Australian struck cross-court for the nick. It rolled and Dittmar held match ball on the man he had never beaten.

He served and, unbelievably, Jahangir struck back with the same shot. Dittmar retrieved, rallied and finished it with a forehand volley intercept that died before Jahangir as he tried to sprint to the back.

It was a match to stand for. To stand, to clap and to cheer and the cheers did ring out as Dittmar walked grimly to the final.

Jahangir was out and the big Australian had at last joined the elite group of players who had defeated the great champion.

Asked how many times it felt like Jahangir had beaten him, Dittmar replied, 'It felt like 100 times.'

But there was no joy in the triumph. The cheers, applause and congratulations washed over him. For the next day was Jansher. 'I'm on form and I've got one to go,' he said.

The battle started with 108 shots and a let. They fought for early supremacy, Jansher was tense. His game open, Dittmar settled well, controlled the pace of the game, dominated with the volley and moved the ball at will. He was severe on all but the tightest shots, moving his opposition short with touch drops and following up with sharp volleys.

The game had been closed down. There was nothing the young Pakistani could do but run. Dittmar pushed the straight drops and drives in tight to the side and when Jansher went high, he pulled down with delicate attacking volleys.

It all looked so comfortable. But then it changed. Suddenly the finishing line wasn't so close, even at 2-0 up. Back came Jansher to level and eventually take the final as Dittmar ran out of gas.

'Losing isn't enjoyable,' Dittmar said of his final loss. 'I'm sick of it.'

8

Boxing Clever On Court

RODNEY EYLES (AUSTRALIA)
1997 World Open Final, Petaling Jaya, Malaysia
Beat Peter Nicol 15-11, 15-12, 15-12

AS THE years went on and world titles passed by, I was slowly coming to terms with the fact that the dream may never happen. By 1997, I really put a lot of pressure on myself to win the title. I had been extremely close to becoming world number one in December of the previous year; Jansher Khan and I were in a two-horse race and the disappointment of not reaching the top weighed on my mind.

I went over everything in my game: physically, mentally, nutrition, strength and conditioning. I knew that I would have been happy if I retired the next day knowing that I put everything into the game.

From a young age I did a fair bit of boxing to hone my fitness. I was always in the ring and any opportunity to work with a boxing coach gave me clarity alongside my squash. After all, there are a lot of similar aspects with the two sports: quick foot movement, good hand speed, to be controlled and not to be too aggressive, when to attack and when to pull out.

I had many memorable sparring sessions with all walks of life and because of this I never felt fazed going into battle on a squash court, in as much as I knew that I would never get knocked out!

I used different kinds of cross-training to keep my squash alive. I always enjoyed the running as I had to back up long matches, even though I liked the attacking side of squash.

It is a totally different scene in a boxing club. I remember being involved with one such club – I'd probably give the game away if I named people and places if I revealed more – where they didn't let me use any other equipment for five weeks until they thought I could use the rope properly. Suddenly I would be on the speedy ball, then get to hit the heavy bag. Then one day a trainer asked if there was a volunteer sparring partner available.

I put my hand up and the next thing I know my gloves are being laced and he's asking me a series of questions about what I did. At the time, I was world number two at this particular club and I told him I didn't do too much as I wanted to keep my career quiet.

Reebok were sponsoring me at the time. I could have had the best boxing shoes, gloves and shorts but I purchased the cheapest, most tatty equipment available. Sticking out like a sore thumb was not my plan here.

The trainer kept on asking questions. After we had eventually got round to the point where he was suggesting that I was actually a criminal, I then told him I played professional squash. 'How good?' he said. 'Well I'm number two in the world,' I replied. 'Make sure you keep your hands up,' he said, lacing the last glove!

We got chatting afterwards and I soon started sparring with boxers who could go 12 rounds and wanted to keep the punches flowing. I wasn't as quick as the better guys, but I could stay involved throughout.

This really re-energised and enhanced my squash. The sport comes across as aggressive and for me, I was trying to build up an aura which stated to my opponents, 'This is my court, my pay cheque and my business.'

That's not to say it was all rosy in the boxing environs. Most of the time I would be on tour and I wouldn't see people for several months. I do remember one incident where I was having a tough spar in a controlled environment with coaches. I drew a bit of claret by opening up his eyes and nose and he was a bit aggressive in the car park afterwards.

'I suppose I won't see you for a while now,' he told me. 'I'll be back,' I countered. 'You can have your opportunity then.' He said a few choice words and when I came back the trainer must have got his level up a few notches as he duly gave me a good old clean-up. But it wasn't as if it was in a barbaric environment, except that back then I would be sparring without a head guard, only a mouth guard.

So, during my 16 years on tour, you could say I met people from all walks of life. The game had given me so much, but now was the time to ask myself some questions about my game.

I knew I had some problems with my movement into the front-right-hand corner on my forehand side. At the time I was based in Bermuda and there were a couple of tennis players who were also there, one of them being Pat Cash and a mutual friend of his, who was involved in the biomechanics and technical aspects of the sport.

Back then, Australia was pretty advanced in sports science, whereas squash was lacking in that department. One evening over a barbecue, I had told him that I really struggled on some movement aspects. So we went down to the tennis court and he suggested opening my stance a little bit and playing the ball like a tennis shot. I played some squash shots off my right leg and he then told me to transfer it to the squash court given that I had more speed doing it.

There were players doing it on tour, but they were probably unaware of what they were doing. It was unorthodox. They weren't taught to move like that, they were just smooth movers, whereas now it's part of the game.

It was like teaching myself to walk again. I did a lot of ghosting and movement by myself on a private court before going back on tour. It wasn't easy; I endured a lot of losses, my ranking dipped three places from world number two.

But in the bigger picture I was gearing up for the World Championships. People were questioning me, while I didn't want to make excuses to the doubters that I was working on technical changes. Deep down, though, I knew I was persevering, even though I did have feelings to call it a day.

I have to laugh, but I had this dream before the worlds. None of my family, apart from my wife who was usually with me at the majors, had seen me play on tour before, my parents or my brother. As that year's event was in Kuala Lumpur, my dream saw me phone my brother to ask him to travel over and support me.

I had been living in Bermuda and thought that it was about time I had family support. The next morning I let the answer machine go and it was my brother saying that he too had a dream about coming to watch me play in the World Championships! So he ended up flying in and I was very fortunate to have him there.

I had played Jansher at the Brisbane Junior Open prior to the world juniors. The match lasted two hours over five games and although I won, it was certainly evident that there was a new era of Pakistanis coming through.

Come the World Junior Championships he cut me to shreds in the final. I don't know if it was a combination of nerves and the pressure of playing in my home town, but I was like a deer caught in headlights.

Yet, I didn't know I was in the presence of true greatness. But it didn't take long for him to have an effect on the senior game when he won the World Championships the following year.

For me, it was a case of slowly building myself up the rankings. I got up to world number six by the time

I was aged 21 before a string of injuries came into the equation, including two back operations.

For me, I tried to chase Jansher down for many, many years throughout my career, but I just couldn't beat him. The closest I had come was when I was two-love up holding match balls in Paris and couldn't close it out.

I then had a match against Jansher on a back court at the Portuguese Open one year. This time he was two games up holding match balls and I came back to beat him over two hours in five games. For me, that was my best win, even though I could barely get up for the final the next day.

I remember the main draw being put up in the hotel we were all staying at in the capital. In the end, there were personal issues as to why Jansher couldn't play. But the form players of that year were really England's Peter Marshall and Jonathon Power, the Canadian who was pretty out there at the time and claimed that he was going to win it, and Peter Nicol, the Scotsman who was more humble about it and went about his own business.

I had barely won anything that year and had no chance of winning, even though I was top seed for the event. However, it turned out that the players I eventually played in my run had all beaten me at some point throughout the year.

I remember playing my first round match, heading back to the hotel and only seeing myself on the next spot in the lobby. I made a conscious effort to not look any further than that.

In the end, I dropped only two games on the way to the final, against South African Craig Wapnick and, in the semi-finals, against Marshall, who had beaten my compatriot Brett Martin as a qualifier in the first round. It was far from a huge shock though. Even though Peter was a qualifier that year, he was a formidable opponent and he had just come back to the world tour after two years out with chronic fatigue syndrome.

So it was a surprise to most people that week that I reached the final. But I had Geoff Hunt in my corner as coach; most of the Australian team were there, as there was a great team culture amongst us back then, while I had my family watching on.

I'd had lots of physical, two-hour matches with Nicol before. I had cramped multiple times, but our final was one of those days where I found the ball going a couple of extra millimetres tighter than they normally would.

The backhand volley drop was working especially well, the finishing forehand was good, the defensive lobs were working perfectly. Everything seemed to be snowballing in my favour as the match developed. It was still a tight match, but I still seemed to have a buffer.

Being a left-hander, my game plan concentrated on Peter's backhand. The forehand wasn't my strength but I was starting now to feel comfortable on that side. He wasn't able to attack it as much as he wanted to, so my added disguise on the shot left Peter fewer chances to capitalise. It meant that I had more chances on my forehand, my favoured side, to finish off more rallies.

It was a calculated, aggressive shot, whereby I had plenty of straight, short shots and the glass court always paid dividends with attacking. Of course, setting that up with tight length was key, too.

However, one of the significant factors for everything coming together had actually come when we went on court before. The MC came up to me and said that I would be walking out first. I told him, 'No, you're going to have to ask Peter to walk out first as I'm the higher-seeded player here.'

From a psychological point of view I needed for him to walk out first. I wanted him to challenge me. On paper I was the seeded player, but the MC soon came back and said Peter wanted to walk out second.

The mind games had already started. At the time I really felt that I had to stamp my presence on the title even though I didn't own it. For me, Peter had to be the challenger.

The music came on, the spotlights went up and I had got my way: I came out second and I gave Peter a quick glance in the process.

Still, there was a massive amount of respect for Peter. He was a fabulous player and we had some great battles. I remember one match that went the distance in Hong Kong where we both ran ourselves into the ground.

In the dressing room, he was in the other corner and I remember leaning over and I put my thumbs up at Peter, even though I had lost. It felt so good to play like that and it was a pleasure to be on the same court. I felt for him a year later when he failed to win the world title. I remember sending him a note saying that he would win it one day.

When I got back to Bermuda I remember pushing the answer machine button and there was another tennis player, Pat Rafter, congratulating me on my win. I remained good friends with him for a good few years after that.

Now Pat is revered in Australia, and if you ask anyone who their favourite sportsperson is, the likelihood is that he would get into the top three every time. He is so well respected so that was pretty cool.

And today? Well, I still love coaching and any time I get the opportunity to play someone, regardless of their level of standard, I will give them a game. After all, it is the greatest game of all.

◊ ◊ ◊

Eyewitness: How the *Daily Telegraph*'s DJ Rutnagur reported it

Rodney Eyles, of Australia, prevented a first British win in the World Open Championship when he beat Scotland's Peter Nicol 15-11, 15-12, 15-12 in yesterday's final. 'It is a dream come true,' the new champion, who was runner-up last year, said.

On stepping off the court, Eyles, 30, rushed to the stands to be embraced by his fiancée, Michelle, and his brother, Michael. But waiting to congratulate him when he returned to his courtside seat was Mohibullah Khan, the brother of Jansher, last year's champion, who is here as Pakistan's coach. The gesture touched Eyles no end.

Eyles was the top seed as he was ranked No 2 when the draw was made. But so indifferent has his form been this season that he was the least fancied of the main contenders. Moreover, he had lost to Nicol the last time they met, only a fortnight ago in Kuwait.

But it was very different yesterday. Lasting only 49 minutes, the final was the shortest since 1984, when Jahangir Khan beat Qamar Zaman in Karachi. But it was not as one-sided for Nicol was at Eyles's heels well after the half-way stage of every game.

The Australian struck 28 winners, a remarkable tally considering that, with the cooling system turned down, the court was a lot livelier than in earlier rounds.

As in Saturday's semi-final against England's unseeded Peter Marshall, whom he beat 10-15, 15-8, 15-8, 15-6, Eyles's main weapon was his short game. He played his drops, volleyed and off the floor, with a magnificent touch. But there was a marked Australian flavour in the power with which he volleyed and drove, cracking a formidably strong wrist.

9

I Handed Over My Bandana And Said, 'That's Me Done'

SARAH FITZ-GERALD (Australia)
1998 World Championship Final, Stuttgart
Beat Michelle Martin 10–8, 9–7, 2–9, 3–9, 10–9

A FELLOW Australian and having grown up playing against one another from under-13 juniors through our years at the Australian Institute of Sport in Brisbane and finally on the professional tour, Michelle Martin was very much one of my rivals in 1998. She was a Sydney girl, I was from Melbourne.

We were 'mates' in our early days and spent a lot of time in each other's company, but you can't have lunch together and hang out once you start to climb the rankings. We kept meeting in finals over a five-year period as world number one and two, and the fact that we grew to have different personalities as well made for a difficult friendship.

Life on court was mentally and emotionally very different for each of us. For me, I was committee member, then chairwoman and finally President of WISPA while Michelle was travelling with her uncle or her brother to events. Playing the Australian Open in Melbourne, the score was 1-1 and I was leading in the third when thoughts started entering my head about the event, business, home town and I lost the match which gave Michelle the world number one ranking once again.

Going into the World Championship Final in Stuttgart, Germany, I was annoyed at losing to her earlier in the year in my home town in front of family and friends. I felt I was able to beat her. I was fit and doing all the right training when I made a mental decision that I was going to win that day. I went into the match feeling relaxed, prepared and ready to go.

I had gone through the early rounds winning in straight games and by the time I reached the semi-finals I was up against my friend and great competitor Sue Wright. Sue was in great shape, but I fortunately had something mentally over her as I had beaten her right from juniors, except the once, when I lost in five in an exhibition tournament in the south of England. Once again I beat my friend and set up my place in the final.

The glass court venue looked amazing as we played on a newly designed court with a new lighting system, making it look very new age and streamlined. The earlier rounds had been played on the outskirts of the city at a great venue, but it was in an industrial area. The crowd were noisy and hoping for a classic final between these two rivals, who were destined to meet once again.

Back at my home base at Caversham, Berkshire, my coach, Mike Johnson, led a group of Aussies through consistent training leading up to the World Championships or any event they competed: six days a week – racket work in the morning and match or fitness sessions in the afternoon.

As late as 1998, we were doing multiple court sprints, running and sprints on the treadmill, ghosting and weights. It was a good ritual. Mike would do all the training with us too.

My game was based on power and volleys and it showed in my style of play. Fast pace, attack and take the ball early. I would volley anything naturally and would be constantly looking to volley any shot at every opportunity.

Meanwhile, Michelle had been working with her brother [Rodney, a fellow pro] and they had made some changes – a more open stance or left foot approach on backhand and it seemed to me the plan was to either shut me down or make me move differently due to the open stance – which I found interesting and wasn't afraid of. All I could think was, 'Go for it, it's my best side and one I am most comfortable with, so you can play me there however you like.'

My game was all about pace, taking the ball early, volleying, hitting the back corners, then waiting for the loose one or the one they had to lift a little and I could go in and attack.

So, I won the first two games, but the last few rallies in the second were tough and hurt me physically. The third slipped by me quickly as I had walked back on to court a little fatigued and stressed by this knowledge.

By the time I walked on for the fourth I had recovered mentally and physically. I said to myself I was going to win and was fully prepared to do so. But then came a situation only a few points in when I tripped over Michelle's foot. My ball might have been a bit short and due to her new backhand open stance I got a racket close to my face, then somehow tripped on her left foot trying to get out of the way and ended up sliding on my backside from the backhand across to the forehand side of the court.

The referee gave her a stroke. I got a shock at the fall and the decision was enough to rattle my brain. Things began to unravel quickly and I got totally chopped again in the fourth. Rhythm and concentration were gone. So we were going to a decider.

But my brain was still gone. Nothing was working and no matter how hard I tried to refocus, the disastrous third and fourth games were dominating my thoughts and decision making. I was taking the easy option and playing boasts at the wrong time and hoping for drop shot winners.

At 8-2 down I managed to make a decision to save my dignity and to show I was capable of at least going down with a worthy fight. 'Make her earn the last point.' So suddenly my brain kicked into gear and I hit length, got all her balls back into play, didn't attempt a winner when receiving and, importantly, I relaxed and started to play squash again.

All I had in my mind was to hit the back corners. The ploy worked. The score was creeping slowly back.

'Eight-four. Hand-out. Stroke, yes let.' Every time I was receiving, I kept thinking the same thing: make her earn the point.

At 8-5, serving from the left box I glanced at Michelle and thought I noticed a look of panic and her eyes seemed a little wider. So I repeated my new mantra every rally: 'make her earn the point'. The points kept coming my way.

At 8-8, the crowd were going wild, but I could hardly hear. This is also the moment when a player often regains their poise. Then it happened. I could hardly believe it. After clawing myself back to 8-8, Michelle hacked out a backhand boast which was travelling awkwardly. As it bounced I couldn't work out the timing or its movement – either try to hit it before or after the side wall. In the end I had no choice and had to swing as the ball was stuck to the side wall. I clubbed it and it went nowhere.

Later on in my career, if I ever felt myself getting tense I had learnt to put myself back at Caversham where I was most relaxed. I would picture myself on Court 2 playing my mate Rick. Immediately, I could feel my shoulders drop, my mind relax and I could find my rhythm.

I learnt to use simple words like 'fight' or 'move up'. They had an impact inasmuch as reminding me the result would come if I fought. And if I fought hard, that result would probably go my way. I would relax and my racket would flow, allowing me to stand up on the ball, moving forward on the T.

At match point down I repeated my mantra, got the hand-out, and snuck another point to level at 9-9. Once again from the left box, I glanced at Michelle, took a breath and served. From the front of the court I hit a backhand cross court and somehow Michelle missed it when she hit the side wall with her racket and the ball went nowhere. The world title was mine.

I was stunned. I turned and all I could think was, 'Oh my God.' I was so chuffed that I had saved eight match balls to win. The crowd were on their feet, the noise was deafening. They had just witnessed a Houdini.

'It's the difference between knowing and believing.'

Sometimes players wake up and try to convince themselves that they will win a certain match, but after Stuttgart I learnt the true meaning of that saying.

◊ ◊ ◊

I suppose it's pretty rare to see someone making that much of a comeback with today's point-per-rally scoring. I remember Jahangir Khan saying once that he loved traditional scoring because you had never lost until it's match ball and match.

For the old hand-in, hand-out scoring, I still had a lot of respect. There was the fitness and the mental element to get the hand-out. You certainly had to play a little bit differently on the old scoring. There was defence and then you could attack on your serve, but it also depended on personalities.

And as much as Australia were doing well in world squash, in both individual and teams, it was hard to get noticed in the press. We were up against Lleyton Hewitt, Ian Thorpe, Cathy Freeman, the Oarsome

Foursome [the all-dominating men's rowing coxless four crew], the Australian rugby team.

By 2002, I had filled my trophy cabinet in July by winning that year's Commonwealth Games in Manchester, which felt like a huge weight had been lifted off my shoulders. Two years earlier, when coming back from knee surgery, I set myself some goals: win the worlds in Melbourne, get to world number one, reach 60 women's tour titles and win the British, Australian and Commonwealth Games. It wasn't until I won in Melbourne, when the press enlightened me of the fact that I had equalled the great Susan Devoy's record of four world titles that people kept saying, 'Go for five.'

However, once the Commonwealth Games were over, I found it difficult to train, assert my aggression and find my competitiveness. I was emotional and moody, yet I still entered into the 2002 World Championships in Qatar.

All the players flew in a couple of days before the event, while I decided to only go the day before. During the night England had terrible weather and massive high winds. In the morning I arrived at Heathrow, checked my bags and the World Championship trophy in, cleared customs, and checked my gate to watch in horror as the departure board changed in front of my eyes. Every flight read as cancelled. It appeared I was going to miss my first round match.

My mindset was one that I was destined not to play, and all I could do was smile. I phoned Jonah Barrington, who I was doing some court work with at the time, and I explained my situation with a laugh.

He scolded me slightly, 'You figure out how to get down there.'

The organisers had to shuffle the draw times a little bit in the hope Heathrow would reopen and I could catch a plane to Doha. I managed a stand-by seat to Dubai, then had to convince UAE customs that I needed a one-way ticket on the next flight to Doha. I had no clothes and no training gear as my luggage was lost somewhere out the back of Heathrow, but fortunately I had my racket and shoes. I was borrowing Nick Taylor's training t-shirt, Lee Beachill's training shorts, Isabelle Stoehr's bra and socks, Tania Bailey's skirt and a sports top I bought at Heathrow. I had to ask squash photographer Steve Line not to take any photos of me as I had none of my sponsors on me.

While preparing for my first round match against a Belgian player, who was obviously hoping for a walkover, I pulled my shoes out of my racket bag, to find a brand new left shoe and an old right one. Somehow I mixed them up while packing. Isabelle sat there laughing as we both realised in wonder at how I was getting through all this. I remember saying, 'It's just playing, I've still got my racket.'

I guess over time as a professional you learn that if you have your shoes and racket you can pretty well play anywhere, in any conditions, it doesn't matter what you're wearing. It's not like your legs or your brain has stopped working. So I just got on with it.

Paul Walters, my partner and manager, arrived for the second round and bought some spare match clothes but no training clothes, underclothes or casual clothes. So my routine of borrowing everyone's kit for training carried on.

I had a slight hiccup in my semi-final with England's Linda Charman, when she changed the pace so much that I lost my rhythm and in turn it rattled my cage. I had a panic attack and envisioned another French Open Final of hard grind which I certainly didn't want. After a bit of a battle with my thoughts, Paul managed to set me straight and I started pushing the pace again to take control and win in five.

I had wanted to win well in the semi-finals to pass the message on to my final opponent that 'Sarah Fitz was on fire'. The plan was suddenly a little shaky. From memory, it was after the semi-final that I was informed by the press my ranking had dropped to world number two as the new ranking list came out during the tournament. I had played and won too many events which hurt my average and so hearing this was just another thing to add to my mental state and list of disasters associated with this event.

I stomped around for a while, took a shower and soon found out the other semi-final was also turning into a battle. Carol Owens, my childhood Aussie rival now playing for New Zealand, and Natalie Pohrer (née Grainger) were going at each other and heading to a fifth game also.

This livened up my spirits as I wanted Natalie to push Carol as I envisioned a long and tough match if Carol reached the final as second seed. A crowd had gathered by the TV set as Natalie took the fourth convincingly. We all discussed the outcome of the fifth and dissected the rallies. When Carol took a big lead, my mind refocused on the fact I would play my nemesis after all. When Natalie finally won, I felt relief as her style of play and a different opponent eased my rattled mind after all the dilemmas I had experienced – and the fact my luggage still had not arrived from London.

Finally I got word that my bags had turned up that night, so off I went to the airport and picked them up myself. I didn't want the drama of waiting for the airline to deliver them to the hotel or any further disasters.

On the day of the final, I was 2-0 up and battling it out in the third when the air conditioning just stopped coping with the heat and amount of bodies in the arena. My feet kept slipping when trying to hit the ball and the side walls were covered in condensation too. I appealed to the referee, changed shoes, yet no one would accept there was an issue, as Natalie was dealing with the situation better and went on to win the third game. Eventually, in the fourth, when Natalie went to move and landed hard on the floor, the referee finally stopped play. The arena was cleared for about 30 minutes, until the temperature and humidity levels were right again, and we continued our match.

The momentum had shifted in Natalie's favour before the break, but I managed to turn it around after a few rallies and went on to to win 10-8, 9-3, 7-9, 9-7 for my fifth world title.

And having given the trophy to tour director Andrew Shelley only a few hours before the final, with enough time for staff to polish it, the trophy was being presented back to me again. I was mentally stuffed now. I gave my bandana to Andrew and told him, 'That's me done.'

I elected to stop playing on the tour and I knew I had gone back to world number one, was current world champion, British Open and Australian Open champion and Commonwealth Games gold medallist. My name remained at number one for a few months, with the agreement that once I dropped from top spot, my name was to be removed from the ranking list.

So, I had won my fifth world title after such weird and amazing circumstances. What a relief considering the mental state I was in only a few weeks earlier. Only a handful of people knew what I had been going through.

Eyewitness: How *Squash Player* reported it

'Give that match to a sports psychologist to explain,' was one seasoned observer's comment. It was the match of the year, no doubt about it, perhaps the women's match of all time. Either player could have won the 1998 world title. It was a match that fluctuated dramatically. But why? *Squash Player Magazine* risked asking the difficult questions.

Let's be blunt, it was a disastrous year for Sarah Fitz-Gerald – until Stuttgart. The world champion really had her nose rubbed in it. In the world Grand Prix in Hurghada, Egypt, she lost to Michelle Martin in four and never really had her game together. Rival Martin went on to collect the silverware at the British Open and the Commonwealth Games and beat Fitz-Gerald in every event except the Citroen Classic in Parsdorf, a consolation prize that can be put down as a not unfamiliar motivational blip for Martin following her British Open triumph.

'I wasn't ready in Hurghada,' explained Fitz-Gerald. 'I thought I would save it for the British but I put too much pressure on myself. I've got to learn to relax.

'In Kuala Lumpur in 1986 I was relaxed. Each day I woke up and I was zoomed in. I just got into the semis and took it from there. I look back and think, "Why can't I play like that?"

'In the Commonwealth Games I got thumped. It's part of the game. She put in the training and you have to give her credit for that.

'I've been trying in the last few months to sort my brain out and I knew that this was the tournament I had to get it together in. I sort of half did, half didn't.

'I fight with myself in my mind. I think too much. If you're focused you supposedly don't know what is going on and I can end up sitting there saying, "Drive into a corner" to myself and if I concentrate on that I forget everything else.

'I play guys all the time and play at a higher pace than you would with women. I stand up to it but it's when your mind starts to let you think. That's where my let-down is.'

Perhaps a sports psychologist would say that for a top performance mental strategy should be positive, focused and, ideally for an instinctive player like Fitz-Gerald, effortless and automatic. Too many unfocused thoughts could perhaps lead to negative thinking and loss of concentration.

'At two-love I started thinking too much,' she said. 'Too much stuff comes into my brain. When you're focused you do things instinctively. At one point I played a drop shot and it was at the wrong time. I thought, "You're just going to run your ass off to get this back." I didn't see the point. She hit a cross court and I just kept running and ran straight out of the door. I just wanted to get off. It was diabolical. I figured I would just have to win the fifth.'

Fitz-Gerald had come back before against Martin but it was a rare thing. She often started the better but the confidence would slowly ebb away to be replaced by tension, and the search for points would become a little more frantic. Martin would get in front more easily and mistakes would creep in. Perhaps the memory of those losses was one of the things that got in her mind.

In New York last year, however, Fitz-Gerald came back in the fifth. She said, 'I was 6-2 down and I remember thinking, "I'm not going to give in to you easily," and I won 10-9. That flashed through my mind. I know everyone thinks that when you're playing you are meant to be totally focused, but the thoughts that come into your head are amazing.'

Strangely at match ball in the World Championships the pressure reversed. This is one little exciting aspect of our sport that traditional scoring allows. The pressure is on the player holding match ball to win this big point. Now the decision is whether to be cautious, to take risks or to be flash. Points can be wasted and sometimes players can fluctuate wildly between these different options.

Sometimes the receiver, burdened with tension, can relax, play better, play with determination and so can start a comeback.

Thoughts flashed through Fitz-Gerald's mind. 'New York shot through my mind and I wondered whether it was possible to come back from 8-2 down. All I was trying to do was keep her on there and make her work – and the points kept on ticking over.' It was a difficult year but it changed in those few minutes.

Were you focused in that comeback? 'I don't know if focused is the right word. I knew what I was trying to do, which was make her work for it. It's funny; I should have been trying to do that from the first point. At 2-8 I relaxed and started to do what I knew was correct. Some of the points came so easily.'

It happens frequently that players get back on level terms and then lose...

'That happened to her in the first. When I came back in the fifth I decided to keep the ball in play. I remember thinking that it was amazing.'

That moment in squash history changed the year for Fitz-Gerald. She was world champion again; champion by a hair's breadth but the title was undeniably hers.

It had been a difficult year on the circuit, Martin had gained the ascendancy but Fitz-Gerald was not operating at near her potential.

It is a strange relationship, friends in junior squash at the Australian Institute of Sport in Brisbane, touring companions in their early days on the circuit, colleagues in the Australian team and now rivals at the top of the sport. It is not a bitter rivalry but one that necessitates a kind of personal separation.

The rivalry started in the juniors where Fitz-Gerald was the outstanding player, winning the National

Under-13 Championships when she was just ten. She won the under-19 title twice and lost once. When the AIS opened, Fitz-Gerald moved from the Star of the Sea Ladies' College in Melbourne to start her six years in Brisbane. She was chaperoned on tour by 16-time British Open champion, Heather McKay.

It took her ten years on the circuit to reach her full potential in a peak performance in Kuala Lumpur in 1986. She retained the title in Sydney a year later by beating Martin, a player who two years earlier she would have expected to lose to.

Travelling is something she loves and she meets people easily, a useful skill she employs as president of the women's tour.

Travelling and training doesn't leave much time for hobbies although she enjoys photography. Her collection of albums covers memories from across the world. She chose four pictures to blow up and adorn her walls: a houseboat from Kariba in Zimbabwe, St Mark's Square in Venice with the pigeons, the blue waters in the Bahamas and the old Inca cities at Machu Picchu in Peru.

Fitz-Gerald still loves travelling. She will be on the circuit for a while yet, continuing her fascinating rivalry with Martin. These two are well out in front – Martin the supreme professional, Fitz-Gerald the rhythmic instinctive player of rare talent.

Future battles loom. It has been a difficult year for Fitz-Gerald but at the end of it she can say she clutches the world trophy. 'This makes up for the year. I have the title.'

10

Annihilation, Magic And Power

JONATHON POWER
1998 World Open Final, Doha
Beat Peter Nicol 15–17, 15–7, 15–9, 15–10

THIS WAS the tournament where I became world champion and world number one. This was what it is all about, the relief of that moment I will always cherish. From growing up, into the early throes of a professional career, you then come to the realisation that you have reached the point you have sacrificed so much for all of those years.

Before 1996, Peter Nicol was top four in the world and I was ranked 50. He beat me a number of times and we were nowhere near the same level. In 1996, at the Tournament of Champions in New York, I beat Pete for the first time and then I won six or seven times in a row. I kind of had his number.

Then the Commonwealth Games came in 1998, one of the biggest events before the World

Championships. Back then I didn't really know what the Commonwealths meant. I certainly didn't rate it as a major tournament and I didn't put that much into it.

I went on vacation two weeks prior to the Games in Malaysia – and as a result Pete certainly got some confidence from beating me to gold in the final. He then beat me again before the World Championships, at a time when I thought I was on top of my game. Pete clearly had other ideas and had worked a few things out, that's for sure.

There was no isolated preparation – as there still is now – we went from tournament to tournament, week to week. As a result, there was tension leading up to Doha. In my mind, there were only two guys who could win that year: myself or Pete. We were in the finals of pretty much every tournament that year and this was going to be the first time we were playing a World Championship together. You couldn't pick who was going to win and it was certainly the height of our rivalry together.

Back then, I always travelled together with Graham Ryding, my compatriot who reached a high of world number ten in his career. For Doha, I also took Mike Way with me, my coach at the time, which was rare as I usually travelled alone to events.

We were all staying in the same room and by luck of the draw, Graham and I were pitted against each other in the second round. We had hit together for 20 years, had played in the finals of the Canadian National Championships every year and it was a tension-filled room.

Leading up to that, it was all about the match with Graham. Even though we had separate rooms in our suite, we were still together and it was a bizarre experience. But I ended up beating Graham quite quickly. He wasn't in the moment and I was playing pretty well.

Amr Barada, the tough Egyptian, was next up. He was number three in the world, but was ranked sixth when it was time for the draw. That was a tough one: to play the world number three in the quarter-finals of the Worlds. It was like playing a local, with the whole crowd pro-Egyptian. Again, I played well. So much so that I rate it as the best match I ever played.

I annihilated him. We were playing to the-then first-to-15. He only won ten points in the whole match and he could hardly score a point.

When you are having the best game ever, there's not one thing you can do to highlight any weaknesses. My movement was at its peak, I got on the ball so early, every drop was going into the nick and every length was getting glued to the wall.

It was one of those days when everything was working, especially when you have an explosive and fast game.

During the tournament I was certainly gaining confidence with every match, to the point of overconfidence in terms of my behaviour. I was so focused on my half of the draw that I had no idea how Pete was getting on or who he was playing. Back then we didn't speak to each other anyway. In 1998 it was a real fractured rivalry. We have come a long way since and we are good now.

So suddenly there was Pete in the semi-final against Belgium's Stefan Casteleyn. I was up against Anthony Hill, the Australian, in the other. And here's a fun thing: Stefan, Anthony and myself all shared a flat together in Amsterdam where we were training.

Anthony and I were good buddies and we had played each other so many times that I felt he knew how things would work out in our match. It meant that Pete and I were going to fight for the world title.

Pete was so strong mentally. He dug in and was so good on defence before making you work for points. It was a great contrast in styles. I was certainly fragile and intensely competitive, but intensely unpredictable at the same time.

So even though Pete was my chief threat, I was my own worst enemy. My on-court antics started when I was eight years old, so you could say I was my biggest rival!

When you're sharing the same space, the match has a certain shape, you kind of know what to expect. And Pete certainly knew what to expect. Not that the final had any niggles. There weren't that many calls or anything out of the ordinary. Yes, there was questioning with the referees on some calls, but that was about it.

All my ducks were lining up in a row in the way of movement, the comfort of my coach, having my buddy Graham there. Everything was in order and they needed to be if you wanted to go through the tournament. There were so many positives.

The first game was incredibly hard from the off. It was corner-to-corner, played at a brutal pace on a very quick court. It was a game that broke the match. I lost it 17-15 and you would have thought it would be bad for me. And it was; I was panicking. I had worked him like crazy, yet I was vomiting in between games already. The opener was that tough.

But I had put so much into his legs, thanks to being able to get on the ball early that, at 5-2 up in the second, Pete didn't turn for, or run for the return.

I will remember the shot: I held and snapped a cross-court shot. He could have gone back and dug in to get it – like he had done ever since I had started playing him – but when he didn't, I knew then that I had broken him.

The next two games were won fairly convincingly and I won it on a lucky nick in the back of the service box. I threw the racket and such was my jubilation I could well have jumped 15 feet in the air. As it was, I ran up the wall instead. I then left straight for the airport, leaving the trophy with a cleaning lady.

I never kept any trophies, even though this was my first world title. Am I surprised I only won one? Not really, because of the two years at the start of the new millennium when they didn't hold the World Championships.

The following year I won the first game in a match against Barada before he bust my knee. David Palmer, the Australian, hit me in the eye when I was almost 2-0 up. He went on to win it in 2002. Unfortunately, freak accidents seemed to get in the way.

I was in my own little bubble during my career. I never read any media and never realised people called me 'The Wizard' or what people thought about me.

Azam Khan, pictured here in 1961 at the British Open, is considered one of the finest rackets players of all time

Australia's unrivalled Heather McKay — won 16 consecutive British Open titles between 1962 and 1977

Jonah Barrington, left, and Geoff Hunt go into battle once more during the 1972 British Open final

Hunt, the methodical Australian, on his way to an eighth British Open crown in 1980

Pakistan's great Jahangir Khan: the longest unbeaten run in sport, at over five years and 555 matches

Ross Norman's 1986 World Championship win ended Jahangir Khan's record

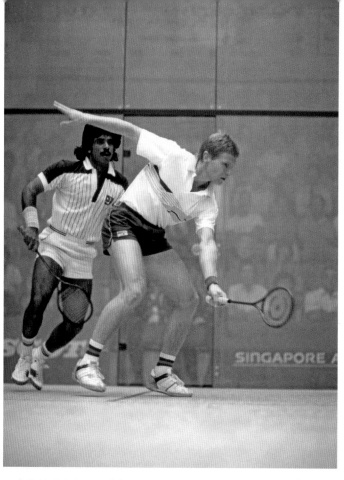

Chris Dittmar, of Australia, faced the challenge of playing both Jahangir and Jansher Khan in the space of 24 hours

Rodney Eyles, right, held off a stiff world title challenge from Scotland's Peter Nicol in 1997

Sarah Fitz-Gerald holds aloft the 1998 world crown after a sizzling comeback in Stuttgart

Canadian Jonathon Power was in magical form during his world title success in Doha, 1998

Celebrations abound for France's Thierry Lincou against England's Lee Beachill in 2004

England's Lee Beachill goes vocal at Boston's Symphony Hall in 2005

Peter Nicol, a former Scot, helped England to gold at the 2006 Commonwealth Games in Melbourne

David Palmer, right, closes in on a brilliant come-from-behind win to defeat France's Gregory Gaultier in Cairo

Malaysian squash queen Nicol David's world title win in Belfast signals the start of an unrivalled career in the women's game

James Willstrop, sporting trademark headband, and Nick Matthew's duel at Canary Wharf in 2010 is considered one of the finest matches of recent times

An all-England Commonwealth Games men's singles final in 2014 saw Nick Matthew, in white, defend his title in Glasgow

Egypt's Ramy Ashour, perhaps the greatest player the sport has ever seen

I understood exhibitions, though, and I was good at drawing a crowd into the game. That's a big part of sports entertainment.

The dust started to settle between myself and Peter towards the end of our careers. There is only one guy who ever really understood what you went through from a certain perspective.

And once you get past the competitiveness there is a certain bond that lives on. It was a special time in our lives, so we understood respect and the sacrifices that we both went to.

Eyewitness: How *Squash Player Magazine* reported it...

Jonathon Power was clearly on 'cloud nine' after winning the world squash title for the first time in Qatar – but his bid to return to the skies later that evening were thwarted by a faulty altimeter on his London-bound British Airways jet.

After more than six hours' delay, the flight was eventually abandoned – leaving Power and his fellow passengers to find hotel accommodation in Doha in the early hours of Sunday morning while a replacement plane was sought. Power had taken the squash world by storm by beating Scotland's world No1 and favourite Peter Nicol 15-17 15-7 15-9 15-10 in the 72-minute final to become the first North American world squash champion.

Eager to get to Amsterdam where a party had been laid on by fellow players, including World Championship semi-finalists Anthony Hill and Stefan Casteleyn, Power transferred on to the next available flight to Europe – the midday flight to London, courtesy of event co-sponsors Qatar Airways.

At last the world champion was able to savour the benefits of his new status, and was duly toasted in champagne by the crew during this trouble-free journey. Power's historic victory crowned an epic week at the Khalifa International Squash Complex in Doha where the richest-ever men's world championship, featuring a 64-man draw for the first time since 1987, was staged ten weeks after being moved to Qatar from Bangalore in India.

Nicol was seeking a historic squash 'grand slam' in Qatar, hoping to add a debut world title to the Commonwealth Games and British Open crowns he had secured earlier in the year – the former in his first final win against the Canadian for more than two years.

Power, who beat Nicol in last year's final of the Qatar International on the all-glass court in Doha but has recently lost three successive times to the Scot, was questioned about his game-plan after the final. 'I don't usually have a plan – I just wing it,' responded the charismatic Canadian.

He acknowledged that he has been taking life somewhat more seriously in the last few months, particularly since his setback at the beginning of the year when he injured his ankle playing a fun game of basketball with his father John – 'doing the bonding thing with my Dad,' he said at the time. 'I must start taking more care of my body,' he confided at the post-final press conference.

The ankle problem appeared to have resurfaced during one of the earlier matches, but his later agility belied this. The first time he played without his familiar ankle support was in the final. 'I decided about an hour before the match to do without it – much to the annoyance of my coach Mike Way.'

The new champion was also magnanimous in his praise of his opponent. 'Peter has improved his game enormously over the past year. In last month's Heliopolis Open final, he played a phenomenal game,' said Power.

In his post-presentation speech, Power also paid tribute to sponsors McDonald's and Dunlop, the British racket brand to which his three-year signing was announced in Qatar. 'This is truly the racket of world champions – both of us are using Dunlop,' said the Canadian, referring to women's world champion Sarah Fitz-Gerald.

Power's triumphant return to his homeland will be delayed until Wednesday, as a result of a Dutch league commitment to Amsterdam team Squash City on Tuesday, when he plays Australian Billy Haddrell. 'Whether or not I'll be up for that remains to be seen,' admitted the Amsterdam-bound world champion.

How the final panned out

Power started the final in devastating fashion racing to 6-1, taking the ball early, smacking in low cross courts, hogging the middle, cutting the ball short with drop/kills, and passing his opponent with deceptive drives.

'I don't usually have a plan,' said Power later, 'I go on and wing it.' And wing it he did. Power was flying, dominating the play, Nicol was responding. The early balls kept firing down the court from Power, Nicol was working up and down digging drops out of the front and passing Power with wide cross courts to beat the volley every time Power sent him short.

Power, however, was able to put his opponent short from all parts of the court, shape for a shot, then play another, always angling it away from Nicol, sliding it cross-court across the floor when a straight drive looked likely, pulling Nicol short for a drop and then pushing it long so that Nicol was catapulted back to scrap out of the corners and set up a Power volley.

Power was dominant and in control but then suddenly it all slid away. A stroke started the slide, a forced error off a clinging backhand, an easy forehand volley drop tinned and a no let on a Nicol drive when out of position, saw his opponent stand at game ball, 14-12. Power risked everything with a forehand volley nick at 13-14 but Nicol seized the advantage with a pressure volley and drive to run out the winner, 17-15, after 28 minutes.

Power should have had it. Would that break him? No. Again in the second he raced away with winners to 5-0, Nicol got back to 4-7 then Power's deception twisted and turned him. The first had tired Nicol, his shots went shorter, he counted with drops but Power was onto them punching them away, snapping in kills and passing his opponent with beautifully angled drives to take it 15-7.

Could he keep it up? Would Nicol be able to wear him down? Again in the third Power pushed and pulled his opponent around the court, drops and volley drops played short so easily then deceptive drives that passed his opponent. Nicol was tiring, the third went 15-9, and he fought to stay in touch, down 9-6, 11-8, and then match ball finally came 14-10, another volley nick, a fortunate one, gave him the title, 15-10.

For a tired Nicol 'it was a game too far'; for Power it was his moment. 'I've been focusing and visualising this moment,' he said. Now the sport has a fantastic rivalry between a new world champion and a world number two.

What Power said after his devastating win over Barada

'He has slipped into my number two position in the world,' said Power after a devastating display against world number two Ahmed Barada when he crashed the Egyptian 15-5, 15-2, 15-3 in just 29 minutes.

'I wanted to show him what it's about. He didn't play well but I didn't let him. I played fast and I didn't let him get into a rhythm. I was seeing it early and was onto it keeping him off balance. I was moving well across the court and I cut it off.'

Power volleyed whole successions of balls on end always seeming to angle and fade it away from the Egyptian who in the end was sorely embarrassed. And on a potential final clash with Nicol he said, 'I'm getting fitter. I became overconfident and thought I could rely on my natural ability but he kept improving his game. He has developed his game to beat me and studied videos of me.'

Following six consecutive wins for Power Nicol has come back to win Commonwealth gold, the US Open and the Heliopolis Open. 'I've been working and playing events and I've got to play my game. I dominate the play but he hangs in and breaks me physically and he's stronger mentally,' said Power. One thing Power has in his favour is the court. He likes it, he beat Nicol on it last time and says it suits him.

'We had an epic on here last year and we were both physically spent. If we meet it's going to be ugly,' said Power. Nicol has his own plans. 'I'm world number one and I really want to be world champion as well,' he said.

Eyewitness: How the *Daily Telegraph*'s D.J. Rutnagur reported it

Power piles on pressure as Nicol runs out of steam

For Peter Nicol, 1998 has been bountiful. For most of it he has been ranked No 1 in the world, and his many successes include winning a gold medal in the Commonwealth Games, along with victories in the British Open Championship and the US Open.

But the final tournament of the year brought heartbreak. For the second time in succession, the last hurdle in the Mahindra World Open Championship proved too high for him.

The Scot was beaten 15-17, 15-7, 15-9, 15-10 by Canada's Jonathon Power, who became the first world champion from the New World.

Power is not a stylist, but he is fast on the ball, highly creative and sometimes unorthodox. Dogged in chasing the ball to all corners and resolute in responding to an initial deficit of 1-5, Nicol saved the first game by the skin of his teeth.

But the breakthrough was far from a tonic. The relentless pressure that Power applied had caused Nicol to do more running, twisting and stretching in 28 minutes of that opening game than he would do in all of a long match.

Before the second game – in which Power again seized a big early lead – was half played, Nicol's legs began to be drained of strength and the prospect of defeat loomed larger by the minute.

Indeed, there was a distinct link between the nature of the court and the overwhelming superiority of Power, who had lost his last three matches against Nicol. The Scot mentioned the fact as a reason, rather than an excuse, for his plight.

Power was even more emphatic in saying that the grass court, on which he had also beaten Nicol last year, could not have suited him more if he had it tailor-made.

The Canadian added that the outcome might have been different had the competition been held in Bombay, as originally planned. 'It is hot there and the ball bounces around,' he said. 'That is Peter's scene.'

Power was exultant after the final about a psychological trick he had played on himself.

'It was the first time since I injured myself in February that I competed without an ankle brace,' he said. 'It was an incredibly liberating feeling. It was a mental decision I made and it worked really well.'

Nicol has won tournaments there for two years, beating Jansher Khan on the last occasion.

He said, 'I have to get stronger to compete with Jonathon in these conditions. I think this was one tournament too much and two matches too far for me.

'It's been a busy year and I am putting away my racket for a fortnight. But I will start working on fitness as soon as I'm back home.'

11

'Coping With World Number One Was Horrendous'

LEE BEACHILL
2004 US Open Final, Boston
Beat Peter Nicol 11-8, 11-9, 11-9

GETTING TO world number one was the pinnacle for me. It required so much consistency, especially in my day when there weren't that many points and it required you to take the required amount in the big tournaments that mattered.

There was a period before the build-up to it all and all the talk around it started to become a reality. From a playing point of view, it was horrendous. Every time you stepped on court, it was mentioned. Every time you went off court, it would generally be the first thing that was talked about. So staying focused was hard for me – and it was a draining experience.

Looking back, you can pinpoint quite a few aspects that went your way: a particular draw or key players getting injured before the major tournaments.

I'm a great believer in that you get out what you put in and if you stick to your principles and working hard, then eventually things will work in your favour. I certainly had my fair share of that when I was starting to come through.

My first incident came in my last year of school went I got pneumonia. It was my first setback, which laid me low for three months out of the game. I then contacted salmonella when I was 17, which was a horrible experience. I had just started playing the world tour and I was starting to get some results against higher-ranked players.

I guess at that stage it's the persistence and if you were ever injured or ill, it was all about looking ahead to the next goal. Whether it was getting back on court in two or four weeks, that was the focus, and the rest of it was immaterial at that time. In all, I had three ankle operations, five knee operations, a double hernia, a shoulder operation. That's about all I got away with!

I also had a car crash in 1997 when my car skidded on black ice. I knew I had done something pretty serious. When squash is now your life and you are asking just a few hours later, in the middle of the night, what your chances of playing squash again are, from a mental point of view, it was pretty horrible. It was all I could think about for a long while afterwards.

I played Pete in a league match when I was pretty young. I know that many people didn't put that much emphasis into these matches, but I did. I hated losing and if I could get a win against a top player, be it a practice or league match, then I would do it.

I randomly managed to beat Pete 3-2 and that win gave me so much momentum. My first British Nationals win in 2001 then made me realise that I could put a run together and beat the top players.

I was seeded 13th in that event and there were players like Mark Chaloner and Alex Gough, who were both in the world's top ten at the time. It was a tournament where everything clicked into place. Nick Taylor had beaten Del Harris, one of the world's top players, in the semi-final and I took my chance in the final. Going through the process of winning those types of tournaments was a huge deal at that time.

I also won my first Professional Squash Association men's tour event in North America, a region where I had quite a few successes. I loved playing in front of big crowds and it always got the best out of me. It was always comfortable playing over there and I never felt stressed. The same still goes for James Willstrop, my fellow Pontefract professional, which is funny really given that we are generally seen as two of the quietest players on court who just got on with it.

That was Malcolm's influence from day one. James's dad and my coach, he always instilled that into my game, one based around persistence, concentration and being accurate.

Malcolm was brilliant at telling me that distracting myself and getting involved with referees and players was counter-productive. Not only that, he had a big ethos of making his players good to watch. So around that time there were some pretty volatile characters so

I found a way to counterbalance that and get the best out of myself.

So, heading to Boston for the 2004 US Open, there was much to be positive about. It was a city I always liked and the Symphony Hall is a striking venue.

At the top of the rankings there were so many competitive players at the top. There were a host of players who could beat each other – Jonathon Power, John White, Pete Nicol, Willstrop, Nick Matthew and Amr Shabana – and trying to predict any event was near-on impossible.

It was all about round after round and hoping you would come out the other end unscathed. It really was about consistency and I rarely lost to anyone I shouldn't have. Ultimately, it was what paid off for me.

As far as world number one went, whoever won between myself and Pete at the US Open in 1998, in Boston, would take top spot.

I have been such good friends with Pete for a long time. He was one player I never felt nervous going on court with. I always looked forward to our games, even though he gave me a good few beatings over time. They were hugely enjoyable games and there was nothing in them that would be difficult to take.

I remember playing the first few rallies and thinking that the ball was going exactly where I wanted it to. It was all about accuracy and this was key, considering that, physically, I was a fraction of a percentage behind the top four in the world.

I had to limit their abilities to expose myself to them. If I could hit accurately, I could control the pace of the game and create opportunities to finish off points. I was striking it so well in the final and I seemed to have this ability to control Pete, whose major strength was the physicality of wearing you down.

In the third game, I just hit shot after shot and the scoreboard starting going in my favour. As soon as that happened, my first thoughts were that I could really win this. But that was my hindrance, and from then on the final became a physical one. The match turned and Pete started to make less errors.

The rally that took me to match ball was ridiculously hard. I think Pete, struggling to get one back, dived into the back corner and he smacked it straight out of court into the venue's organ pipes.

On match ball, there were some considerable thoughts going through my mind. The match ended on a stroke. I was confused and wondering what the referee had just said. I wish it hadn't ended on a stroke decision, but there was so much riding on that one point that I certainly wasn't going to go off court and demand that we play a let!

I had become the first Englishman to become world number one, even though Pete had become the first Briton to reach top spot, before switching allegiances to England from the Scotland flag.

It was a strange experience to be honest. For me, squash was all about other people. Whether I had won, lost or drawn, going home was always a big part of it, while the reaction of seeing other people's joy far outranked the feat of actually doing it myself.

I wasn't running around the streets of Boston or diving across my hotel room. I was more interested in just getting home and seeing the reactions of those people – my dad, Malcolm, the people of Pontefract who had supported me throughout my career – which was the real buzz.

The pressure of getting to world number one and dealing with it is very difficult to explain to anyone. When you do eventually get there, suddenly there is that expectation to win every time with your rivals chasing you down, which was something I found hard to accept.

Everyone talking about you now winning a tournament before you've even hit a ball is also hard to accept. Players like Pete and David Palmer were exceptionally good at dealing with these issues, the expectation of then going on to win.

It is something that I perhaps didn't have or deal with properly. But it is a unique, personal thing and hopefully I was able to say now that I gave other players an enormous amount of respect. Getting to world number one certainly didn't change that.

12

Doing The Double In Doha

THIERRY LINCOU (France)
2004 World Championship Final, Doha
Beat Lee Beachill 5–11, 11–2, 2–11, 12–10, 11–8

THE CHANGE of scoring to point-per-rally to 11 really fitted into my game, much more so than the 15 scoring, which had been introduced at the 1989 World Championships.

My endurance levels weren't as good as some of the top guys on tour, whereas I was more offensive and aggressive on the T. My game plan was to try and pick the pace up; in that way the 11 scoring was better for me in terms of taking the ball earlier.

Perhaps I was the main beneficiary of the scoring changes. I had a great year and it was the perfect build-up to the last tournament of the year, the World Championships in Qatar.

When I lost the world final in Pakistan the previous year against Amr Shabana, the result did give me the world number one spot. When I reached the semi-finals I learned that I had reached one of my goals, and perhaps this was my downfall in the final.

So I started 2004 as the world's best player, but without having lifted one 'big one'. A few months later I was really happy as changes started to happen. I started with the Super Series Finals at Broadgate in London, the end-of-season finals which saw me win my first big tournament.

My second came at the Hong Kong Open in August and I played brilliantly all the way through, beating Nick Matthew 3-0 in the final. I then beat the great Jonathon Power on his home patch at the Canadian Open in Toronto. A final win in the UK then really built my confidence up.

By the time it came to Qatar, I overheard a television interview where Alex Gough, a former top ten player, was asked at the opening ceremony who he thought would win. I was surprised at the answer. 'Well, Thierry will win this one,' said Alex. But maybe at this time I was the best player, with the best shape and in the best form.

I loved the court in Qatar, which seemed to be around for ages until a new court was installed for the 2014 World Championships. One of the first worlds I played, I was aged 21 and I remember playing Anthony Hill, of Australia. I had three match balls against him and I really screwed up with three bad hits into the tin.

Apart from that, I fell in love with the court. I went there twice a year for competitions and I always used to reach the last eight or semi-finals. It was a fast, flat court, the ball always stayed in the corners and you always got reward for tight shots.

It was an unforgiving court, too. I remember speaking to Power and we both agreed that you had to be so fit to have any chance of a title. It was fast, but dead and you had to move well.

But I got off to a good start that year. I beat Englishman Bradley Ball 3-0 in my opening match and then faced my fellow Frenchman, Gregory Gaultier. It was a tricky, tricky match but I had the mental edge at 2-1 when I pulled away.

Part of my strategy was to wear players down and sometimes losing a game was no bad thing. As the game went on, I would really build it up and become a machine.

So I was comfortable with my fitness and by the time I had beaten Australia's Anthony Ricketts 3-2, having been 2-0 up, things were looking good.

I faced Graham Ryding in the last four, a player who was super-confident having overcome Peter Nicol in four games in the quarters. The Canadian was a player who loved to attack with the boast. On that court, it was so hard to see the boast off the glass walls and the balls used to die in the front. To say he created a lot of damage with that shot was an understatement during the tournament. He nearly got me too. I saved one match ball against him before winning 6-11, 11-3, 11-4, 7-11, 11-10. Another match in five!

On the point that gave me match ball I hit a rolling nick at the back on a lucky bounce from a cross-court shot. He was so gutted that he hit a tin from the volley to give me the match.

I knew then that this was my tournament, that somehow the world title was meant to be. Everything seemed to fall on my side and that ball that hit the nick summed it up.

I was, however, so tense throughout that semi-final. I lost my confidence and I was scared of losing. He was clearly the underdog and it proved tricky for me. I told myself ahead of the final that I would play better, not to be afraid and be more relaxed.

After each match, during my stretching I would dissect the game, what went right and wrong. I would then totally switch off and forget about the match completely. I would think about anything except squash. I thought about it as just another tournament to stem off the pressure.

The year before, I had loads of radio and television interviews in Lahore and I spent up a lot of energy. I think it's what partially cost me the title. But this time I was prepared in how to best perform. The tournament had got the top two seeds in the final. But this was going to be tough: Lee Beachill was world number one, he had won the US Open and was playing at his best in the top half of the draw.

Even if I had a good record against him, it was going to be a battle of precision on the length. He could hit perfect, crisp shots on both sides, which he complemented with cross-court shots from the back and a great hold at the front, especially on the backhand. He didn't talk too much on court. For me, it was way better than to come up against the English spirit and mentality, one where you played fair and there were few arguments too.

But I knew I had to move in on his shots. If he controlled the pace, he could get the shots too tight on the walls and he was a likely world champion.

It perhaps explained the slightly weird scoring in the opening two games: 5-11 and 11-2. I wanted to move him so much, but I couldn't do it. He was holding his authority on the T and he always had time to hold. I had to get in front of him and get him further away from the ball.

I began to find some openings, even though he raced away with the third, 11-2. Where was this match heading? It was becoming an unforgiving court and I was wasting so much energy in trying to find the right balance of play. He was becoming so strong and steady.

Into the fourth, I got him to play longer rallies in a slower game. And I still had to save my second match ball of the tournament! I didn't freak out, though. I really surprised myself and I really went for the volley drops. It wasn't a risk though. I was there to win and I remained positive; if I could have won the fourth then I knew I could break him.

I did, I was relieved and it was the turning point. I had played him so many times before that I knew once I got into his head then I had him. He knew I had a strong finish and I think he knew that it would be hard for him.

I think that I was more tired than I felt, but I always had a little cushion in the decider. I was far from controlling it, but I still had the capacity to play relaxed. I kept on moving, twisting and turning him and he didn't like to lunge being a tall guy. He hit the tin on match ball.

Yes, I had been happy to be world number one (the first player from a non-Commonwealth country to do so) in Lahore, but was more than disappointed to lose the world final. I could have done the double, but I always felt something was missing. In France, being a runner-up or a world champion was night and day.

Going all the way in 2004 was my time. I came off court and Jahangir Khan, who had won so many world titles, was the first to congratulate me.

I remember after the match ball I stayed on court and walked around the court, not really realising the moment. I was so focused on the game plan and trying to break him down that I was drained on the final point. With the win, I had got back to world number one. I had done the double and I had learned some big lessons in Doha. I knew that reaching semi-finals and finals was never enough. You had to go all the way to the end.

How I Got Fit...

I would go into the Alps in the summer time to really peak for the new season. I would stay in Tignes or Alpe d'Huez for two weeks on an altitude squash court and by the end I would have that extra gear. I had an extra gear because of it and I would feel much more comfortable doing this. I would always feel great going back down to sea level afterwards.

I was a big fan of ghosting during my career. It was my trademark on tour and I was able to be quick and explosive because of it. I worked on it for many years and I was able to be really sharp on the T and get in and out of corners with a much more fluid movement with years of ghosting under my belt. It felt natural and effortless, like I was dancing.

A typical ghosting session for me would last six minutes. One minute per corner: two at the front, two at the back and a volley to the side of the T. It would be high-intensity and I would go for the full six minutes. I would then vary the length with shorter, 30 second bursts, to mirror what it might be like in a match.

Eyewitness: How the *Daily Telegraph* reported it

Leading 10-9 in the fourth game, Yorkshire's Lee Beachill last night stood one point away from becoming the first Englishman to win the World Open Championship. The distinction eluded him, however, and the title went instead to France's Thierry Lincou.

His 5-11, 11-2, 2-11, 12-10, 11-8 victory in 83 minutes made Lincou, who briefly topped the world rankings earlier this year, the first player from continental Europe to win the title.

From the manner in which Lincou, the losing finalist last year and the second seed, conceded the first and third games to Beachill he seemed destined to suffer another disappointment.

The Frenchman's errors, as much as the inspiration and discipline with which Beachill played, seemed to have set the match on course to peter out.

Yet it went on to provide the most exciting finish since the Kuala Lumpur final in 1989, when Jansher Khan made a dramatic recovery to beat Chris Dittmar.

It was not that Beachill's game went into decline. Instead, Lincou established his authority with tight, incisive squash to emerge a worthy champion.

13

From Meltdowns To Melbourne Glory

PETER NICOL (ENGLAND)
2006 Commonwealth Games Final, Melbourne
Beat David Palmer 9-5, 10-8, 4-9, 9-2

MELBOURNE'S Commonwealth Games was a unique period in my career. I was 31 years old and up until then I had never planned anything other than trying to be the best I could possibly be at every tournament I entered, other than World and British Opens.

Eighteen months out from the Commonwealths, I thought to myself that I couldn't keep playing all these events and set about reducing my schedule on three things: the individual and world teams in 2005 and then peaking for the Commonwealths in 2006.

I had never done this before and it was interesting going through the 2004/05 season and then having a long break and almost going back to basics in terms of my training.

I started from scratch and did a lot of training with the England squad at the time, as well as spending time with Pete Jennifer, a fellow pro. I had a great group and a plan I set about to achieve.

At that time, I was going through a phase when I wasn't being as professional as I could be. My lifestyle had changed a lot and I wasn't as focused as I had been.

I had done it with not much rest and not many injuries for such a long period. The way that I was mentally, I had given so much to everything every time that I was done in a way and couldn't continue doing it.

Rivals must have wondered how I was going to play. At times, I could play wonderfully, on other occasions I would be fairly average, or even terrible. It was perhaps a stage where it was a good opportunity for others to play me due to my inconsistency.

As with most things, I didn't care what people thought, I just wanted to be fit and ready for the task ahead. What was so special for me was that the Commonwealth final was going to be my last match that I was going to care about. It was my whole life, my whole career and also unfinished business with England Squash from the 2002 Commonwealth Games.

I had transferred over to play for England from Scotland and had picked up a silver and gold, but it was disappointing as they had expected me to win the gold. In my first Games for England, I lost to Jonathon Power 9-4, 4-9, 9-0, 9-0 in the men's singles final.

Playing for Scotland, I had become world champion in 1999. A year later, I picked up a shin injury and Scottish Squash had been forced to cut my income for four months. I still had to pay Neil Harvey, my long-term coach, and I was becoming disillusioned with the national governing body.

I had spent close to 20 years living in London and I could qualify to play for England under the residency rule. But changing allegiance to play for England was a difficult time. I hardly slept the night before the press conference where I revealed why I was doing it. The news made the front pages of the broadsheets and I received death threats.

Being funded by England Squash allowed me to use the raft of free coaches, physiotherapists, psychologists and video analysis on their world-class performance programme. It is fair to say that it benefitted me a lot: I won six tour titles in my first year as an England player and also regained the world No.1 spot the following January, a position I held unopposed for two seasons.

Four years on from the 2002 Commonwealths, Melbourne was to be a special time as I wanted to spend time in Australia with the people who had got me to this point: David Pearson, my coach, and Stafford Murray, the video analyst and friend, and 'Fingers' Phil Newton, the physio. I just remember this wonderful build-up to Melbourne with the years and years of investment from both sides.

I flew in from New York to Melbourne, where I lost to Greg Gaultier 3-2 in the quarter-finals of the Tournament of Champions at Grand Central Terminus. One of the reasons I probably retired was because I wouldn't have to play the likes of Greg again!

He was younger, fitter and when we had long matches he would generally win.

I was happy with my form though and was happy not to win the event. I had a couple of good nights out in New York, where incidentally I met my partner, Jessica, and then it was two weeks back to business and being prepared.

We were there for a long time before the opening ceremony and it was kind of surreal being in a bubble for ten days before moving into the village. Essentially, we were in limbo. And I was in dire form as well. I couldn't move on court and Lee Beachill, my doubles partner, was taking the endless piss out of me too.

I had a couple of meltdowns during the period on the bus and it was a chance for more endless fun from my team-mates. I was being petulant, being sulky but it was down to the fact that this event was so big for me. I had peaked in New York and I had expected to continue that form instead of realising that I might dip and hit form again.

With no disrespect to the players, I had a really good draw. That dawned on me when Nick Matthew and James Willstrop played each other in the quarter-finals and played a phenomenally long and brilliant match, which finished up 3-2. I played the winner, Nick, in the semi-final.

I had played Canada's Graham Ryding in the quarter-final. Now Graham was a good player, but he had only ever beaten me once and I wasn't going to let him beat me. The next day I pitched up and I knew that Nick was slightly jaded after an hour. Things fell into place and I had some fortune which allowed me to play into the event.

So I was delighted that I was then going to face one of the great Australians, David Palmer, in the final. A Commonwealth Games final in Australia, I knew it was going to be a great occasion, in front of a partisan crowd.

As with everything else, I was part of a Games village which was all English and then you are segregated from the crowds by coming through the back entrance, so I never noticed the extra hype that day. It was certainly different from other squash tournaments whereby players are usually integrated with the court and crowd.

The times that I've always known I was going to win was when I have walked on to court with sheer total relaxation. More than I am relaxed in day-to-day life. It is a weird thing to describe. Some people may call it the zone, but it's not. It's just the walk, waiting to go, having a chat with the flagbearer or people in the stands. I remember tossing my racket up and down and walking out, feeling like I was having a beer on a Sunday afternoon.

I knew then that I was going to win; it was just a case of what was going to happen. I wouldn't get tired because there was no nervous energy in my body. All that was going to happen was it was going to take as long as it took to win. It was a lovely feeling.

In between the knock-up in the first game, David Pearson came over, whereas another coach, Paul Carter, had previously done so. There is a clip on the television which shows me laughing and pointing to the crowd, where I am telling David, 'That's nice of you. All week you've been sitting in the stands and now you come for the show match!' This was before the first game, but it was that kind of atmosphere!

I remember my father had once said to me that when you get to the place, do it properly. I was going to. I was fully prepared and was going to do the best I could.

Looking into my corner I saw my group and all the players, including Lee, who didn't agree with my moving to England from Scotland originally being the proud Yorkshireman that he is. It didn't change how he was to me – it was his opinion after all – and he soon became my best friend on tour. Knowing he was now in my corner urging me to win, having not made the final himself, was very special.

I can't remember the first two games, though I won them both. They were long and tough and Palmer was doing what he normally did: look to volley, be physical, be aggressive and assertive. I looked to counter that as much as possible and then volley and lift and work him and make sure he wasn't getting away with the points.

What was crucial was that I needed to win the second. He was making a push and by the time he won the third, people thought I was doing too much work. They were worried. I could see it.

Sometimes squash people see a player doing a lot of work, but fail to see the opponent is doing just the same volume. As long as I was playing a fluid and relaxed game it wasn't hurting me, so I wasn't worried.

Speaking to people afterwards, they were terrified I was going to fall over.

In the fourth, I was fully invested in the moment. It meant everything to me as the winning line drew closer. It was such a special moment and it is the only part of my squash career that I have ever watched again – and continue to watch.

As a sportsperson, you are kind of driven by certain deficiencies in your personality. I was incredibly shy and I used squash for confidence from a very young age. As I became a professional and drove myself forward I continued to use squash. Around events, people would never have thought I was shy. So I didn't really want this to continue, hence the reason to cut down on events.

It was hand-in, hand-out at 5-2 for what seemed like an age. But when I got to 6-2, it allowed me to show off all this emotion, to let it all out and be confident to express that this was who I was. You never saw Palmer fall over and the moment he did so going into one at the front corner, when he was forced on to his knees, that was the moment I pumped the fist and knew I had him.

It was the first time I had expressed myself on court in those final points. It wasn't an easy time for me and perhaps this was the reason why I was so emotional. I had been thinking hard about the reasons why I had become a squash player, what had happened in my life up until that point and what I would do after my career finished.

I had to do a drugs test after all the interviews. It took around two to three hours and Lee stayed with me throughout as we were due to play the first round of the doubles the next day.

We eventually went to this bar close to midnight and after some of the other players left, we went upstairs to a private section with the England support staff. It was a moment when everyone said something one by one, what it all meant, what it was all about. It was highly emotional and I felt really proud to be part of an England group to make that kind of a moment happen.

Eyewitness: How *Squash Player Magazine* reported it...

Playing in his third consecutive Commonwealth Games final, Peter Nicol was unfazed by the patriotic home crowd at the Melbourne Sports and Aquatic Centre, as he added another gold to the one he had claimed in Kuala Lumpur in 1998. Both men had enjoyed strong semi-final wins to progress to the gold medal match. And this being the Commonwealth Games, it wasn't simply a case of one opponent against another.

This was the might of the old empire against the best the home nation had to offer. This was the white shirt of Nicol against the green shorts and gold top of Palmer. England v Australia yet again in the squash – and for the umpteenth time in these Games.

From an early stage in the match, Nicol took control of proceedings. He dominated for large parts of the first game, winning 9-5. The second game was much closer but, unfortunately for Palmer, ended in the same result. 10-8 to Nicol.

With the gold medal almost around his neck, Nicol led early in the third game before the Australian managed to fight his way back into the match. He levelled the game at 3-3 and moved ahead once the players had returned to the court after the match was stopped for the blood rule against Nicol.

Finally, the passionate home crowd began to stir. The more they roared, the better Palmer played. He took the game 9-4.

Yet any fears of a heroic Australian comeback quickly subsided.

Nicol reassumed control in the fourth game, as his opponent made more and more errors. At one point, Palmer even flung himself across the court, throwing his racket at the ball, but to no avail.

With every point won, Nicol clenched his fists and shouted 'c'mon'. A 3-1 score became 4-1; 5-2 became 6-2. And, not long after, it was 9-2. Game over. Gold medal won.

At the end, Nicol sunk to his knees, thumped his fists against the glass and clutched his head in his hands, scarcely able to believe what he had achieved.

'It meant everything to me,' Nicol revealed immediately after the match.

'It was one of the last tournaments I'm ever going to play in, and certainly the biggest one I'm going to play in at the end of my career.

'I was very, very tired going into that fourth game, but I think I played the best game of my career.'

14

The Cairo Comeback

DAVID PALMER
2006 World Championship Final, Cairo
Beat Gregory Gaultier 9–11, 9–11, 11–9, 16–14, 11–2

WINNING FINALS is not all about playing your best squash; it's about winning the match. Cairo was a great example: the match didn't pan out the way I wanted it to, it was winning that final point and that was what I was good at in my career.

Looking back, it was a pretty relaxed period of my life, even though I didn't know it at the time. Squash perhaps wasn't my main focus with our first daughter being born and I must have gone to Egypt in a different frame of mind. I was not only playing for myself any more. More relaxed, I simply performed better than anyone over the week. It was an amazing feeling.

With the tournaments out at the Giza Pyramids, they always did a live TV draw. As I was number two seed and Amr Shabana was top seed, we were the only players known in the draw and so I was invited out. They played most of the matches at the Cairo Stadium in the city and only a couple of us were playing on the iconic glass court out in the sands.

Playing at the pyramids is one of the best spots to play squash. However it did make practising pretty tough and it was virtually impossible to play in the day because it was so hot and you can't see the ball at that time. It was more for fun to look at your surroundings and say you hit a ball on a glass court in front of the pyramids.

It wasn't ideal as the warm-up areas weren't great, as well as it being so sandy. But it was all worth it as the images were lasting and the promotion of the sport was heightened – especially when the World Championships were played there.

I had previously played at the worlds in 1999 when they were first played there. I had lost in five games to my compatriot Anthony Hill, which at the time was a pretty good result for me.

But I had a pretty good run thereafter. I won my first world title in 2002. A year later I hurt my abductor and lost in the last eight. It was frustrating in 2004 when there was controversy on the last point against Lee Beachill in the semi-finals. He was 2-1 up and hit a volley into the tin. I was running for it and I stopped, but the referees saw it as good and Lee then had match point.

It was devastating for me as Thierry Lincou then won the next day, but I'd had a pretty good record against him, so I felt that was one I had let go –

especially after seeing that video replay of the ball hitting the tin. In 2005, I then lost in the final to Egypt's Amr Shabana.

In 2006, my daughter was born and the year turned out to be a pretty unique one. Typically, I would stay in Europe and prepare for the new season. That year, though, was one of the first times that I went back to Australia after the last tournament in the UK in April.

Normally World Championships are held late on in the year, but the Cairo event was early September and there was only one event leading up to it. It was winter back in Australia, but that didn't stop me from putting in a tough training programme ahead of the worlds. I was back at my home town in Lithgow in New South Wales, a mountainous area, and I was out there with my dad, an inspiration to me, so we would go mountain biking a lot too.

We would do a bunch of hill sprints, multiple beep tests, and then get back on the bike and repeat the process. Over the years I had several players visit me and we would go up this monster of a hill, Hassans Walls, where the lookout point is 1,100m above sea level.

Shaun Moxham, my coach, had focused my attention ahead of Cairo: every time I rode up a mountain was a match at the World Championships and getting to the top signified lifting the trophy. In my mental preparations, he used that reference a lot.

Fitness-wise, it was one of the strongest points of my career and even though I was probably lacking match practice, my movement and speed was at its peak.

At the time, I was nicknamed 'The Marine', which I think was coined by my friend and tour MC, Robert Edwards. I had a reputation as being one of the fittest, if not the fittest player on the world tour. I suppose it was based on my total attitude towards the game; my preparation, my dedication and my never-give-up mentality, coupled with all the training my two coaches had put into me over the years.

I was ready for Cairo and when the draw came out I was pretty happy with it. The one I had to be careful of was Ong Beng Hee, the Malaysian, in the second round. I found him a tough player to beat over the years, so my focus with Shaun was to make sure I won both those first two games 3-0, knowing that I had compatriot Anthony Ricketts in the quarter-finals.

We grew up together and he was a couple of years younger than me. I had a lot of respect for him and had some great battles which was no different from the Australian rivalries of Chris Dittmar and Rodney Martin down the years.

I had a good track record and always felt I had fractionally the better mental edge. But he was equally fit and so determined, but I got through in four after losing the first.

Now I was up against Thierry, the champion from 2004. He was known for a slow start sometimes and our matches usually took a similar pattern. And it was no different in Cairo where I won the first 11-2. If I won the second, most times I would go on to victory. But if I lost it, the match would take a different turn.

It was a tough battle, even though I won in four and ran away with it in the end. Mine was also the first semi-final on that day, a situation I always enjoyed, knowing that in this position my match hadn't gone to five and lasted two hours on court. I was in a good place.

So perhaps I was surprised to then see Gregory Gaultier reach the final, after the Frenchman beat Shabana, the top seed, defending champion and local hope who had beaten me the previous year.

Now Gaultier was capable of achieving absolutely anything in the game. He was nowhere near as consistent as he would prove to be later on, but he could certainly put together a streak where he could win a major tournament like this.

I didn't watch the other semi-final apart from the closing stages in my hotel room. Mentally, I was preparing to play Shabana all week in the final, purely because of the Egyptian factor. The final could have gone either way. He might use the home court and crowd to his advantage or perhaps feel the pressure playing in front of so many people.

I remember watching Ahmed Barada, a fellow Egyptian who reached the 1999 final at the pyramids, and how he played three or four times better than when he played on a home court.

Knowing it would be Greg threw me off-track a little bit and the Frenchman took a 2-0 lead in the final. It wasn't me being relaxed, more it was a different mindset having to play Greg rather than Amr in front of the pyramids.

I have analysed the first two games a lot over the years. I was playing well and felt I should have taken one of those games, with both going 11-9 to him.

Going in level to the third would have been much better, but Shaun was telling me how well I was playing and how few mistakes I was making.

The goal now was to win the third – which I did, I had to – and perhaps I took the foot off the pedal in the fourth, believing that I could now win the title. Greg pushed on and took a lead, while I was becoming frustrated.

There were a lot of lets and he was simply handling the situation. There were a few movement issues between us, which was getting in my head – and next thing I know he is at 10-6 and holding four match balls for his first world title.

At that point I remember him being confident that he would win it. He went for a couple of quick winners to finish it off, but I won those in a relatively short space of time. If there had been some longer rallies at 10-6 perhaps the outcome would have been different, but his bad mistakes were letting me back in. A tight volley drop winner then gave me some momentum and within a minute I was back to 9-10.

All of a sudden, his expression and his body language changed. Sensing the situation was something that I think I was good at over the years, while having my physio, Patrick and Shaun in my corner really helped, too.

This was it. I knew that we were in a situation where a couple of points could really swing a match. By now, Shaun and Patrick were really encouraging me. 'Come on, let's pick it up now, he's getting really nervous now,' was the thought running through my mind.

There were a couple of decisions that went in my favour, while the referee started to be a bit more severe on Greg and started to give him a few no-lets and gave me a few more strokes.

I now had a one-point lead all the way to winning the fourth 16-14. What a feeling that was to think I had saved all those match balls. Any player in any tournament, let alone a world final, would have nightmares about letting match balls go. But I was still in the match with a chance of winning it.

I quickly got some energy gels inside me and I remember standing up the whole time in between games. That was Shaun's idea, to keep me upright and not relaxing by sitting down.

Walking back on, I was trying to show that I had energy left and had positive body language. When Greg walked back on, his head wasn't in the right place and he had a negative outlook.

My goal was to win the first few points in the decider. In fact I won the first four points and the feeling was utter euphoria. It was an incredible feeling, until he got his first point on the board.

But I got my head down after that. 'Come on,' I said to myself. I then started to put in a dig that I also used throughout my career. 'Come on, I want to be first to six.' Every time in two-point bursts.

Everything was working in my favour. Greg was making a lot of mistakes and it was the way the game was panning out.

All my shots started to work, there were short rallies and he was talking to himself a lot. I sensed he was physically and mentally broken. On the flipside, it gave me a bundle of energy and I started to play faster and faster.

It was as if I really was on that last mountainous sprint up the hill. So much so that I think I was even running to the front of the wall to pick up the ball so I could serve again. I just didn't want to make the same mistake that he did from 8-2 up.

I knew I had him at that point. Even after 100 minutes on court and a long week in Cairo, it was such an adrenaline rush knowing I was going to win it. Even though I wouldn't rate it as one of my best matches, this was certainly my finest achievement; coming from 2-0 down and saving four match balls.

I try to get the message across to a lot of the players I coach now, namely that finals are tricky. Sometimes you don't play your best squash, but finals are about winning that last point. All the top players know that. There is such a difference between winning a tournament (for the confidence, the prize money, the points) compared to being runner-up and receiving half the points, half the prize money and not getting that brilliant feeling of winning a tournament.

How I Got Fit...

There were some unique aspects to the training on court as well which Shaun used to come up with. One of them was called the 'Killer Routine'. He would hit the ball to either side to the back of the court and I would have to volley it, with length, and run back and boast it back up to him.

He was always at the front and he could choose where to put it next. If he put it to the front, then

I would run there and choose whether to put in a straight drop – depending on how balanced I was – before Shaun then chose to put it to the front or back again.

Every time it went to the back I had to volley it to the back then boast again. At the front, wherever Shaun put it I went for the straight drop, unless I felt I was under pressure. If I felt that I was then I would have to lob myself out of trouble. If I did that then I would have to go back and retrieve it myself.

The routine would consist of 10–12 minutes each time and we would do five to six sets of it every time. A lot of my training consisted of doing routines five times in a row to mirror going the distance in a full-length match.

I needed to push myself to the max in each game and I based my game around those theories and the Killer Routine was just one of those.

Eyewitness: *Squash Player*'s Richard Eaton recalls a remarkable world final in front of the pyramids

It was appropriate that the final of the men's World Championship was played before one of the Seven Wonders of the World. This was the most compelling of all the 28 final showdowns since the event was first staged in 1976 – a multi-layered drama with hidden undercurrents and a late twist performed before a great and mysterious landmark.

There was a long and brilliant surge by Gregory Gaultier, a short and dazzling comeback by David Palmer, five thrilling match points, a controversial sequence of refereeing decisions, and a dramatic contrast of styles and characters.

It was as if the immensity of the three Giza pyramids had elevated the players, as well as the pharaoh they were built for, to a higher realm.

It was the disciplined Australian against the expressive Frenchman, the Colossus versus the Imp, and the bravest player in a world final against the unluckiest.

Palmer's victory was, until the five-minute post-script of the final game, by far the less likely result. The final point scored was among the least likely.

The 30-year-old needed every ounce of will and every dash of fortune to survive against a 23-year-old who, until a sudden and disastrous denouement, played irresistibly the best squash of his life.

Palmer also delivered some of the most pleasing quotes about the people around him. His wife had inspired him during their daily webcam chats, his new daughter Kayla had delighted him so much that he dedicated his second world title to her, his dad was with him in spirit when it mattered most, and his opponent was 'probably unfortunate not to have won'.

It was a combination of pater's influence and coach Shaun Moxham's psychology which helped squeeze Palmer through the toughest test of his career.

'Shaun told me to imagine I was not in Cairo, but in my home town of Lithgow,' he said. 'I'm just climbing the mountain with my dad and that's how I take the pressure away.'

But for Palmer to imagine he wasn't where he was took some doing. All around were the most unexpected distractions, often with a sense of things not quite being what they seem.

For the last five kilometres of the winding road around the pyramids, tourist police stood at 50-metre intervals, backs to the road, facing out into the desert, as bizarrely inconspicuous in their bright white uniforms as was the armed motorcycle escort which led us erratically on every horn-honking journey.

Bomb-seeking mirrors were thrust under every vehicle, gruesome photos of a devastated Beirut appeared at the venue entrance alongside happy pictures of Jansher Khan and Peter Nicol and a banner saying 'Lebanon As It Was' oddly substituted the past tense for the present. Time seemed to warp.

Without Moxham's plan to block it all out, the man from New South Wales might never have made it.

15

Why Being At The Top Is The Best Place To Be

NICOL DAVID
2006 World Open Final, Belfast
Beat Natalie Grinham 1-9, 9-7, 3-9, 9-5, 9-2

THE MOMENT that defined my whole squash career came when I was 2-1 down against Australia's Natalie Grinham in the 2006 World Championship Final.

We were both on stage – and performing was certainly how it felt that night – in the beautiful surroundings of the Albert Hall in Belfast, Northern Ireland. It was my first time as a world number one and I was just coming to terms with being at the top of the game. But did I have the right to be there? It was a question I had asked myself throughout the year.

After winning my first world title the previous year in 2005, I lost in the final of the Kuala Lumpur Open back home in Malaysia at the start of the year and then the Commonwealth Games semi-finals in Melbourne.

At the 2005 World Championships, I had to beat Vanessa Atkinson in the semi-finals for me to be world number one in the following month's rankings. There was so much buzz around the sport, especially with the Malaysian public, as it was all new and had yet to really sink in.

It took me a while to get back on my feet as I didn't know how to deal with lots of issues like Malaysia honouring me in lots of different areas. It took time for Malaysians to also understand what was happening. Having a world champion in squash, or any sport for that matter, was so rare.

I had put so many expectations on myself to do well and it took me a while to grasp that fact. It was certainly a tough place to be in, being world number one and world champion, and I was tasked with now bringing back a Commonwealth Games gold medal ahead of defending my world title.

It happened so suddenly and so early on in my career that you have to take some time away from squash and reflect on what I had done so far in the sport and what I can do in the future, instead of digging a hole and putting yourself down.

In terms of rivals, the Grinham sisters – Rachael had been world number one for a few years – were really pushing the barriers and it was a time when I had to think about where I was and who I was as a player.

I'd had a good build-up to the World Championships and I knew that the Grinhams were on form too. If I wanted to defend my title I would have to overcome both sisters too.

They are both so tenacious. I played Rachael in 2004 at the US Open and they have a lot of different plans and styles set up when they play me. But along with my Australian coach, Liz Irving, we always talk about what they might throw at me.

Whatever happened I knew I would be able to stay with Natalie whatever she threw at me. It was going to be very brutal, especially after what we had produced at the Commonwealth Games Final a few months earlier. Sure enough it was one of the longest matches we played, at around 90 minutes.

It was a beautiful setting in Belfast. The glass court was on a stage and you felt like the crowd were with you inside the glass court. At the back of the court there was a huge organ and it gave an extra feeling to the event. It was as if we were the show that night and we were here to entertain. It was special.

As the match progressed, the crowd seemed to get closer and closer. The tension was really high that day; you could feel the energy and you could feel the crowd hanging off every point.

Liz knows me so well that I was always going to put the first game aside after losing it 9-1. I did so and wanted now to have trust in my game plan.

Liz kept me on track, told me the pointers and to make sure that Natalie didn't get an edge. She was slowly trying to creep back into the match after winning that first.

It is one of the great things about Liz. I came over to Amsterdam from Penang in 2003 and I have been coached by her ever since. I think she came over to coach from Australia for only a few months, but she has been there ever since too!

Over time she has changed my movement, my swing and my technique. Back in 2006 it was more an understanding as to what to do with it. Liz had taken apart my game from scratch in a bid to just get me to – three years down the line – understand how everything works and being able to put my game into place at the right time.

It was the starting point for how she wanted my game to develop: a base for good volleying and movement. It is something, still today, that we continue to focus on as we develop game plans, feel on shot selections and options during matches. The difference between 2005 and now is huge.

Now I have the consistency to understand my game, as well as Liz being able to bring in more ideas that she can also offer. It just amazes me what she has in store for me every time I step on court with her. There is always more insight and detail that she picks on and she is the reason for where I am today.

We were playing back then with the old points scoring system (the traditional hand-in, hand-out); that much I remember by the game we both played in the fourth. It went on for just shy of half an hour and it stayed 7-4 for what seemed like an eternity. I won the point, having played several 80- and 90-shot rallies, and we were soon locked at 2-2, with everyone on a high right from the start.

Before the start of the fifth, Liz just said to 'go for it, you have nothing to lose'. I was fired up and played really well and soon I was closing in on my second title.

Before winning the final, I never knew whether taking the world number one spot was my position to take. So for me, 2006 was a real learning process and the World Championships set a benchmark over where I stand in the world of squash.

The moment I lifted the title in Belfast, I knew where my place was and this is what I was here to do. It was a turning point in my career and the realisation dawned on me of knowing that this was my place. I told myself that I was going to keep training and working hard at this level for as long as I can.

Having been world number one ever since, do I now know myself what has got me into the position and how I have managed to maintain it for over 100 months? Well, I think it is a combination of several factors.

I came on to the squash scene at the right time in terms of the funding that Malaysia granted to me, the support from my parents and allowing me to train in Amsterdam on my own and the belief they had in me. Having the right people to assist me and take me to the next level has been a significant factor.

They were there in Belfast and they have been at nearly all my major finals since. Of course, coming from a hot country, they were a little surprised at the cold in Northern Ireland. I remember them nearly being blown off the stairs when they walked off the aeroplane!

Liz has been at the top and knows what it's like to stay at the top, to keep me buzzing and making me want to fight for that next world title bid or tournament win. Even after all this time, there are so many more areas to work on – and that keeps me even more excited.

Ronald has been working with me ever since my first world junior title, a 15-year working relationship in how my body works. He is called the structural integrator and it sounds like he takes my body apart and puts it back into place. It is just like that and I will be ready to go the next day!

Ronald has been so important in my career and being ready for that next match. We train so hard, but at the same time if you get the right recovery you are ready and fresh to go the next day. I have been in a fortunate position where I have back-up, be it psychology or physio, at every turn. Some players have to play through injuries on tour as they don't have the same facilities as me.

I make the most of what I have and I realise the importance of all the roles people have in keeping me fit and solid. Only then can I maintain the way I am and how I can progress. Even today I am feeling the best I have ever been. My body is now conditioned and I know how much it can take to educate the muscles to stay strong over a longer period of time.

Of course I have had moments of doubting myself as a world champion. You have so many other years in between where there have been some tough losses and then getting out of it; to lose in the final of the British Open and then get ready for the World Championships two weeks later. The years have given me the experience to bounce back. It is all about being strong, determined and taking on all the challenges.

I have learnt over time not to get too deep into my losses, but think about what actually happened. It's all in the mind and once a solution has been found it's all about moving forward.

But there's one thing that will always remain with me: the need to know that winning my first world title in 2005 was not just a one-off thing. I just moved forward from there. It struck me coming into 2007 that I wanted to keep pushing as being on top of the world was the best place to be. Why settle for anything else?

Eyewitness: How *Squash Player*'s Richard Eaton reported it

David becomes Goliath

Nicol David sounded a bit surprised. 'One hour and 36 minutes?' she said. 'I think that may be the longest match I've ever played.'

Her five-game win over Natalie Grinham in Belfast's elegant Ulster Hall was certainly the longest match of the 2006 Championships and longest women's world final of all.

Of course, statistics can be misleading. The length of a match sometimes indicates little and can even obscure its essence. But the 96 minutes played by the top-seeded titleholder from Malaysia and the Commonwealth champion from Australia revealed important truths about both.

It was protracted because of the notable tactical plan which Grinham employed, and the competence with which she executed it, not just because the players happened to be well matched.

Grinham set out to hit the ball harder and lower than usual, denying David many chances to volley and setting up a struggle for charge of the centre of the court, a battle of line and length, speed and stamina. She had devised the place because of the manner in which David had been dominating the women's game, with an unbeaten run of more than 30 matches, and it produced tough line and length rallying, characteristic of the men's game a couple of decades ago.

Grinham stuck to these tactics admirably – admirably because it required guts – and they earned her a lead of a game and a 7-5, and got her to within striking distance of winning the match in the fourth game. It was only from 7-5 in the fourth that David took charge, and the victory was more a triumph for her developing mental strength than her developing style.

It is a matter of opinion, however, whether or not it was good to watch. Some newcomers thought it was repetitive; aficionados tended to find it mesmerising. What is certain is that it was uncommon in the women's game.

Maybe no longer. Grinham failed only because she grew slightly more tired than the best athlete in women's squash. She nevertheless succeeded in finding a way to combat the sport's outstanding woman. She herself regarded her loss as a success which may have an interesting bearing on future encounters between the two.

It had all been so intense that David was frozen, unable to leave the court at the end and her beaten opponent graciously helped her away. 'I got so emotional,' she said. 'I didn't realise how much pressure I was under until the end, and then it hit me.'

Though David made impressive strides in 2006, Grinham was accelerating not too far by the end of it. It helped that the world No.4 is based in Amsterdam. She and her Dutch husband-coach Tommy Berden were well placed to observe how David was adding to her game, working with that greatest of all drive-volleyers, Sarah Fitz-Gerald.

16

A Double Marathon At Docklands

JAMES WILLSTROP
Canary Wharf Classic semi-final, London, 2010
Lost to Nick Matthew 11-7, 5-11, 18-20, 11-8,
9-8 (retired)

WHEN PEOPLE talk about aggression and how you have to be evil on squash courts, the Canary Wharf Classic semi-final from 2010 had it in spades. We didn't need to cheat or foul or bad-mouth the opponent. We just played some of the purest squash imaginable, in a match I came away smiling from, despite failing to win it.

Our match was still pretty fresh from the 2009 British Open Final at Manchester when all the problems off court started between myself and Nick.

I had a good run at the North American events leading up to it, where I had beaten Ramy Ashour to win one of my favourite events, the Tournament of Champions at Grand Central in New York. I hadn't really got ill and I got the in-between things right like the training and getting rest from the travel.

I was in good shape and this Canary Wharf event had the baggage of the rivalry with Nick, which goes into every one of our matches. I suppose looking back, it was more pronounced then than it is now because of the British Open the year previously.

We had played each other a few times, but Nick was in a strong position and was expected to win. It was just another one of our matches, but the Canary Wharf match had some added spice as there is extra publicity and the excitement and atmosphere of playing in London gave it an extra lift. If we had played it in Kuwait it wouldn't have had the gravitas as it did that day.

I certainly didn't think heading into the event or even that day that I was going to play the best match I was ever going to be involved in here. It was just another week, preparations had gone well and I was ready for the tournament.

The first game of our semi-final was of a really high quality. I wasn't even caring that I had lost it. It was fine with me; if we can both carry on like that then there's nothing else I can do. If he beat me 3-0 then so be it. But then if I kept playing the way I was, I was bound to get something out of it.

I was having a very positive discussion in between games with Malc, my father and coach. A lot of the time, the mindset is negative when it builds up having lost a game. But this was different and I won the second well, 11-5. Then came a mad third. I had a lot of game balls and I should have won it earlier. It was perhaps the clincher in terms of how the match then panned out. It was a monumental game, though I don't think it quite eclipsed the mammoth 57-minute first game between myself and Greg Gaultier later on in the year in Delhi, but it was long and hard.

Everything was flowing and I was in control of the match at 7-4 up in the fourth. But Nick put in one of his unbelievable digs and came back to take it.

Maybe people were going to write afterwards that this was where I blew it, where the match was lost. Yes, probably, but I didn't think about this later.

The quality was incredible and he produced such good squash to get back at me that this was going to be one of those matches where I couldn't possibly feel disappointed.

At the time, playing all those lengthy rallies, your primary concern is to think how on earth you can break it down, break Nick down. That's the challenge of squash, when you get two players who are going at it full-blooded.

His court coverage at the best of times is top class, but that night it was exceptional. He is so quick and there are very few balls that he can't get back.

Unless you are a Ramy Ashour, you can't just thrash the ball and beat him with winning shots on a consistent basis. Even when I have seen Ramy play Nick, I can see the Egyptian grappling with the situation and trying to find the space to hit the winners.

Nick makes our matches very chess-like when we play. We are both craving the space and it's hard to find. So once I started to get embroiled in rallies like we did in the fourth, questions were being posed, 'How am I going to find the space?' But if you can't find it, don't search for it, just stay with it and speculate and wait for an opportunity. Those were the primary thoughts.

The great Jonah Barrington happened to be on commentary to the side of the court that night. And those who were listening would have remembered him talking about when two players are in this situation it was a case of 'mind versus mind'.

Our matches certainly tapped into Jonah's views and philosophies on squash. It is all about finding that space, the chess-like nature of the sport and you can do only so much with your sharpness of shot and your killer instinct. But when it came to this match, it was all about who could work the geometries to bring the other player to a standstill.

It was just probing squash, with fantastic shot-making. By the end of the fourth, I was certainly aware that we were in this monumental battle: not just in the physical aspect, but also the way it was going playing-wise. I remember Malc not saying much. There was very little said. There didn't need to be and it was all very positive.

On court, the quality remained and we kept on probing. We were playing to such a level that it was always going to take something out of you. I don't say this lightly and I don't say it very often now how well I played, but I knew it was going well.

As the fifth developed we were locked in battle with only a few points left to decide the outcome. A hard rally ensued.

You are making movements and you think to yourself that if you go too far on a stretch, it's all going to unravel. Sometimes you can get over it and sometimes you can't. I just remember that I must have pushed the movement to reach the ball too far, but that was typical as Nick was dragging me into places that I didn't know existed on that court.

I was moving an extra half a yard than any other player would probably take me. I was forced into it, Nick was at the front, I was in trouble and he hit a forehand deep to my backhand side and that was it.

I knew as I made the lunge to the back of the glass that something might happen. I had felt it a couple of times in matches before, where you feel as though the cramp is about to happen.

There was a lot of adrenaline flying around, so I can't remember it being any more painful than other cramping incidents, but anyone who has experienced it will know the after-effects.

It lasted 30 seconds before I could even think about trying to stand. As it was only cramp, I felt as if I could play on and that the match wasn't over just yet. After all, I was three points from victory and a place in the final, with Nick only two away from the win.

I knew it wasn't an injury, but the physios were on straight away. I think they were more alarmed than they needed to be. They were thinking that perhaps I had broken my leg from my agony of having clattered into the back wall, my writhing pain and my subsequent outburst.

Malc was straight on court telling me not to carry on and the physios were still prodding my leg and I was trying to call for calm, still insistent that I could play on.

But players know that once they have cramp, that's it really. The muscle is out of action and it's gone too far. As the seconds ticked, I knew it wasn't going to happen. I would have to do it on one leg and need to hit blinding nicks on every shot, but then there was the possibility of doing more damage.

I warmed down later and I had my team around me. We weren't disheartened. It was actually a lovely feeling. There was no point feeling down, as I felt so good. I wanted to be around people. We had given everything and it was one of those matches where you feel so content with what you've achieved. We train to beat the likes of Ramy Ashour and Gregory Gaultier, but that night the winning became a separate issue.

Yes, it was a hard loss but I really didn't give a shit. Everything was great about the match. We played so freely, there was no niggle on court and it was one of our best matches.

It was a thrill to be there and having played a part in it, despite the loss. I was also thrilled that I didn't have to go on court after 120 minutes to play the final less than 24 hours later. That would have been a disaster and I was certainly breathing a sigh of relief in quite a serious way that I didn't have to play that! It wouldn't have been funny.

Nick Matthew has never received the recognition for that one effort alone. We had produced a breathtaking occasion, one I have compared to marathon runners in the past being a two-hours plus match. Marathon runners need, quite rightly, a six-week rest after clocking that time. I certainly needed that amount of rest after Canary Wharf.

But Nick came out and won the final. He didn't just play, he went and won, beating Gaultier pretty convincingly. Now, that has to be one of the best athletic achievements you can possible imagine to do what he did there.

And if I had won? Well, it would have been a really daunting thing to do. I know that the whole day leading up to the final I would have been thinking that people have paid money to watch the final and I knew my limitations.

However, I am just glad we played a match of that calibre. For one thing, it didn't hold a candle to our British Open Final as it had none of the aggro that left a really nasty taste in my mouth. I really didn't enjoy that experience and I certainly didn't walk away from there smiling, even though we had played a five-game thriller.

Eyewitness: How the *Daily Telegraph* reported it...

James Willstrop's bid for a fourth Canary Wharf Squash Classic title ended in utter agony last night after one of the finest contests in recent memory against compatriot Nick Matthew, the world No.2.

Matthew was leading 11-7, 5-11, 18-20, 11-8 and 9-8 in the fifth after 127 minutes when Willstrop collapsed with thigh cramp at the back of the court and was forced to concede the match, writhing in pain.

Matthew clenched his fist at winning the point but immediately put his hand to his head, understanding the harsh situation of the moment. With no injury time-out in the offing and the physio working hard, Willstrop simply had to play on after the referee concluded cramp.

First physio, then coach – his father, Malcolm – shook their head before Willstrop hugged Matthew. Both realised they had played the finest match of their lives. Compelling? It was only the half of it.

It was no way to end such a physically frenetic game, too – the longest in the Classic's seven-year history. These two players had already met three times this year, with Matthew yet to lose, but Willstrop's tight drops to the front and his rival's unerring ability to grind down his opponent made for a classic encounter.

Willstrop had early leads in every game as he bid to overturn a three-year losing run to the 29-year-old.

A conservative opening from both players paved the way for the match. Flair was replaced by the purist's style – this was far better than that other energy-sapping, two-hour epic seen in last year's British Open Final – and the crowd stayed transfixed for every one of the two hours and seven minutes on court.

After Matthew took the opener, Willstrop attacked from the off in the second as he sent the England No.1 cross court to open up successive 3-0 leads. Matthew did stay in the game, starting with a trademark backhand winner into the nick, but Willstrop managed to hold enough points to level the match.

Lets were being handed out like free Docklands newspapers but that was only part of the story in the third, one of the longest on tour all year. Again Willstrop took an early lead and for the first time the tempo upped as fierce, attacking squash came into play.

Willstrop was playing with better touch to the front – summed up by Matthew's unsuccessful let call when the referee responded with 'too good' – and found himself with three game points at 10-7. Matthew's game came into force at once. Length to the back gave him a game ball at 16-15 but Willstrop eventually found the resolve to clinch it 20-18 after 38 minutes.

The intensity continued for the remainder of the match, as did the question of which player was actually going to muster enough fresh legs to play France's Gregory Gaultier in the final. There simply was no let-up and well into the fifth, Joey Barrington, commentating on Squash TV with Jonah, his father and former great of the world game, was overheard saying, 'You'd think they'd be playing for 10 minutes.'

It remained a lottery until Willstrop was denied a crucial let call at 8-7 down. To say that Matthew had the edge thereafter would be cruel as Willstrop's belief remained intact. His only blemish came courtesy of his left quad – a cruel, cruel way to end another barnstorming battle.

On this evidence the Lawn Tennis Association would be wise to take a trip to Pontefract, the Yorkshire club that coaxed Lee Beachill to world No.1 and home to Willstrop.

There, they would find the reason why England Squash have six players in the world's top 13 and countless more as to why they would fight for a place in any international team event.

Willstrop and Matthew: head to head in 2012

In the space of two years Britain had produced two world number ones who both hailed from Yorkshire, Nick Matthew and James Willstrop. In that time the pair proved a revelation on the PSA World Tour. Up until the US Open – when neither reached the final – the last time either Willstrop or Matthew failed to make the last stage of a tour ranking event came in November 2010, a sensational run of 19 tournaments. That telling statistic told of their stranglehold on the men's game, at a time when Egypt boasted five players in the world's top ten. In 2012, I brought the duo together to talk about their career-long rivalry.

RG: We must first start with that semi-final at the Canary Wharf Classic in 2010. Was it the best match you've both been involved in so far?

Nick Matthew: It had everything. There were times when he was on top and vice versa, a huge tiebreak which had drama, games where I was down and out, full-court squash and the drama with James's cramp [when Willstrop was forced to concede the match in the fifth after 127 minutes]. It was very unusual that two players play as well as that on the same day in an environment like that too. But it came together on that day.

James Willstrop: I think the British Open in 2009 was quality, but Canary Wharf had everything: the rallies and pushing each other to the limits. It was one of those matches. I remember coming off and the cramp was horrible. But, warming down, I was very relaxed about it. There was no point feeling down, as I felt so good. I wanted to be around people. We had given everything and it was one of those matches where you feel so content with what you've achieved. We train to beat the likes of Ramy Ashour and Gregory Gaultier, but that night the winning became a separate issue.

NM: Halfway through the match James had won the third game and I came to my corner and felt like a boxer trying to throw in the towel. I certainly took on multiple personalities during the break. My coach, Neil Guirey, was talking to me, but I don't think anything got through. One minute I was saying to myself, 'Oh well, he's got to beat me one day,' and the next, 'Well, it won't be today.' Those emotions will stick with me. I think he cramped about a second before me, with all those long backhand drop-shots he was producing going just above the tin.

RG: If Canary Wharf had everything, what went wrong at the 2009 British Open Final in Manchester to make it so fraught?

NM: It was a rollercoaster in a different way. Whereas Canary Wharf was a classic virtually every point, this was more of a scrappy affair. It was a dig-in, gritty type of match, where we saw the small confines and gladiatorial nature of the sport. Neither player ever goes out to be confrontational or have needle in any way.

I was getting beaten comfortably. I almost had to gee myself up, perhaps in the wrong way looking back on it. But I just needed something to see me through. We were playing the final at 7pm and an hour earlier we were doing a live chat with Chris Evans on BBC Radio 2. It was an interesting build-up, that's for sure. I remember Chris asking James about banter on court and James said that Nick liked to do this or that. I used to be taught by James's dad, Malcolm, as a Yorkshire junior and his philosophy has always been to play the ball, move out of the way of the opponent and don't fish for strokes. Perhaps the interview was still fresh in my mind, because during the final I remember James not getting out of the way of one shot and I said, 'Did your dad teach you to do that?' There were fumes and the rest is history. Perhaps I have Chris Evans to thank for the win.

JW: I don't really remember the interview or what was said, with it being so close to the final. But when I think of Canary Wharf I feel good about it, less so than the Manchester final. It is always a great achievement to reach the British final. We know it was contentious under the most intense pressure, but I don't look back on it with fond memories. There was a bit more room for niggle perhaps, as it was the bigger tournament, no disrespect to Canary.

RG: The great thing is that this rivalry is not recent. What is your first memory of each other?

JW: I think I was six or seven at the British juniors. I think Nick was there and we might even have played. The rivalry thing, the fact we have gone right back to the beginning and now we have got to number one and two in the world, is a pretty fantastic story, isn't it? As an innocent kid playing Nick, week in, week out, those early Yorkshire teams were also great early memories, with the parents mucking in at weekends.

NM: All I remember was that he was taller than me, even though I was 12 and he was three years younger than me.

RG: Over 20 years on, here we are talking about the best two players in the world.

NM: The second-most-asked question I get asked after why squash isn't in the Olympics is my rivalry with James. However, it is not just about us, as that would be disrespectful to our peers. But the close proximity to where we live, the difference in characters and the matches we've had are certainly what make it. It's important to maximise it, I think, but it's not about being ranked above James. I don't think we would be talking about it if we were world number 14 and 15, would we?

JW: Nick pointed it out in an interview, where we were seeded one and two, and it was another anticipated final between us. But people don't realise how hard the first rounds are. I wouldn't even consider playing Nick until I am there. Yes, we are both at the top, but the depth is getting stronger and we can't take anyone for granted. For us, it's the last thing we think about.

17

From Hospital Bed To Glasgow Gold

NICK MATTHEW
2014 Commonwealth Games Final, Glasgow
Beat James Willstrop 11-9, 8-11, 11-5, 6-11, 11-5

IT WAS a session we had done over a thousand times previously. Quite often, lessons with my coach David Pearson are not the most strenuous type, they are quite technical. Sometimes he would bring in a shot and a ghost, where you would simulate hitting the ball. It was his way of doing a pressure feed.

I was feeling pretty good as I'd had some time off after the British Open in May as I would normally do. I was into my third week of training ahead of the Commonwealth Games, David had been away for a few of them, I had done three weeks on the physical side and so I was keen to get on court with him.

We were working on a routine where perhaps it was two steps to every shot and back to the T. Randomly

I got a sharp pain in my knee. I hobbled around for a couple of minutes and it was almost like I was able to run it off.

Several factors entered my mind. Was I cold? But then again I had warmed up. It was a weird feeling and coming off court I thought I had just tweaked something and a bit of physio would sort it. Unfortunately that wasn't the case.

I saw an English Institute of Sport physio in Sheffield that afternoon, had an appointment with England Squash & Racketball's physio, Jade Leeder, and a knee expert in Manchester the following day. There was swelling, but no real problem was laid out. I was walking okay, but occasionally I would jar it.

A few days later I went to see rock band Kings of Leon play in Sheffield. At one point I was struggling to walk up some venue steps and I literally stumbled into Richard Higgins, the EIS doctor who has worked with Sheffield Wednesday, at the Olympics and with the England under-21 football team. He asked me what the problem was and it was clear that there was an underlying problem beneath the fat pad.

A few more days passed and I was soon advised that I would have to go under the knife within 48 hours, five weeks before the final in Glasgow was due to take place. It was certainly a shock to the system and I remember having a ten-minute wobble on the realisation of surgery.

I had to trust the advice and I admit I was in tears when the doctor rang me. My initial thought was that was it, my Commonwealth dreams gone. Okay, I had won it in 2010, but 2014 was the one I had circled.

Winning a gold medal in your home country was what I had in mind.

I pretty much knew that I wouldn't have a Commonwealth Games again so I had been working with my psychologist and not putting too much attention on Glasgow. When something is your big goal it is a big motivator when it's distant, but as it gets closer it can become a noose around your neck.

The way I said it to Esme, my wife, as surgery loomed was, that 'I was still going to win gold'. It was now up to me to do everything I could to get there after surgery. I was pretty stubborn.

Behind the scenes, while I was recovering in hospital, time was short as a plan was being concocted. There were now under five weeks to go and Jade came to see me in hospital. 'Get some rest, because when you come out, you're not going to have a day off for the next four weeks.'

Even on the weekends I was icing six times per day with a 'game ready' knee-icing machine. The EIS had them, though you had to return them each day. So I managed to borrow one off Jessica Ennis-Hill, who was heavily pregnant at the time and didn't really need hers!

The following Monday, a week after surgery, I started in the gym. There was a happy medium between my physio, Jade, and my strength and conditioning coach at the EIS, Mark Campbell.

He was the one who was pushing me, while Jade held me back. My mentality is more like Mark's but Jade was the one who said that it was the accumulative stuff that you put in rather than improving it day by day.

Mark is a 6ft plus Kiwi and he had to come up with ingenious ways to keep me fit while I was effectively on one leg and hobbling around. The main issue was that it was mostly upper body work that we focused on. Squash players have amazingly fit strong legs but are generally quite light up top. It was during this time that I actually got some kind of beach body with upper body muscles. Usually I had a pigeon chest.

I had given Mark a statement of intent, 'Keep me fit and I'll be fine, the squash will come back dead quick.' So in the following weeks we used a series of machines which Mark adapted for me: rope pulling with a sled attached, single leg cycling, upper body rowing, seated boxing, aqua jogging in the pool, to name but a few.

A lot of sprinters would alternate legs in order to get power through their muscles. Mark would take the pedal off the right side, put a box in its place and then tell me to 'hammer it' with my left leg. To put this into context, cyclists do this exercise with both legs and take it in turns. There was no respite and no light pedalling with one leg. Even moving the pedals was hard. The lactic acid it created meant that it felt my leg was going to explode, while I was walking around in circles at the end of the session.

Mark is brutal at what he does. As an example, when I tore my ankle ligaments six years previously, he flushed out all the bruising in one session. My ankle was black from the operation, but two days later I was in the gym training.

So it was that, two weeks away from the Common-wealths, I was able to start solo training. To say it was frustrating was an understatement. I had to be totally static while it was only for ten minutes, which felt like it lasted ten seconds. We slowly built up the minutes and the steps, leading up to drills before I played a practice match with friend Alister Walker, who plays for Botswana, a day before travelling up to Glasgow.

A few days later I was celebrating the biggest honour in my career. I knew that I was on the shortlist as Team England's flagbearer, but I never realised I would be voted for. When I was called into chef de mission Jan Paterson's office, I had an inkling as to what it might be about, but my brain was working overtime if I had actually done something wrong.

There was no way I wasn't going to go after being nominated. It was a bit of a worry, as before that I had to sit down to take the pressure off for a month or so and this was going to be a long day at the opening ceremony.

Jade had to carry a seat with her around Glasgow that day and all the way to the stadium until we got to the entrance at Celtic Park. Every time we walked ten metres as we wedged towards the stadium, Jade would put the seat down. I think some of the athletes behind me were ready to change their vote, thinking I was some kind of diva!

But carrying the flag beats gold medals and everything else having being nominated. You don't get nominated unless you have been successful.

I was tense, but I tried to look relaxed. If anything it now put some pressure on me as I had to win the men's singles now. It focused the mind even more on my pursuit of gold.

My last competitive match before lining up against Xavier Koenig, a Mauritian solicitor opponent, had come in the final of the British Open in May when I was beaten by Gregory Gaultier.

The early rounds were an opportunity to get ready mentally. But the best thing about the first day was the fact that it was two matches; during my training I had never been on court more than once per day. Further, I had watched myself play more than actual court-time thanks to my psychologist, Mark Bawden, who also works with the England cricket team.

I had spent 15 minutes per day watching videos every other day, the second week I was visualising 20 minutes of actual play, while the third week was planning a process of who I might play.

There were over 1,000 people inside Scotstoun Sports Complex on that first day. It was a nerving occasion for the Mauritian, who ended up forgetting his racket, while the match represented my 100th England cap.

However, the match that gave me impetus came against Scotland's own Alan Clyne in the last 16, a bizarre encounter in as much as we both shared the same birthday so the crowd were being willed on to sing 'Happy Birthday' to us. It created a fine atmosphere. It was also a great test of my fitness and it was a match I called 'walking the dog'; we had done all the planning and now it was a case of letting the dog off the leash and going for it.

A few days later I had overcome Peter Barker in the semi-final to set up yet another clash with James Willstrop, a repeat of the 2010 final.

Now James hadn't publicly announced his hip problems (he was to have surgery soon after the Games), so the fact that we had both reached the final without dropping a game, and with prior issues, was testament to both our mental resolve and the support staff.

All week, I had been spinning a line to the media. 'I am just grateful, as five weeks ago I was on a hospital bed...' In my own head, there was no way I thought that and I hadn't come this far to get a silver medal. It was my way to stay relaxed and I was saying all the right things to take the pressure off.

I knew that James had got emotional after his semi-final win, so subconsciously was he thinking that a medal had at least been guaranteed after overcoming the odds to reach the final?

For me, it was gold or bust, as I woke up on the morning of the final. I thought I'd kept that thought to myself before I realised my dad had been on BBC Five Live telling everyone I wasn't going back to Sheffield without gold. It ruined my plan of going into the final as underdog!

I have a pre-match ritual in finals of surveying the court, taking in who's there, get my eyes in to see what's happening, then there are no surprises when you get out there. I was now aware of the packed crowd and all the Olympic legends who were there that day like Sir Steve Redgrave and Victoria Pendleton.

There was also the backstory between myself and James. We were both good at concentrating on the here and now, so nothing was going to affect us, even though there had always been a bit of tension ever since our 2009 British Open Final.

He is the player I have played against the most in my career, we had both been world number one, both been England number one, national champions, and now we had both been injured. We are different characters, not on each other's Christmas card lists, yet we don't need to be friendly. If it meant that the final was sold out, then long may that continue.

The final fitted the billing. Physically and movement wise we may not have been at our best to rival our match at the Canary Wharf Classic in 2010, but tactically and mentally we were right up there. Canary Wharf was a four-corner match, this was a slightly more cagey affair due to the occasion.

I've had a decent record over James, but there were a few times when he had been up in matches. This time, I felt that he believed that this was the day he would end the record.

He was too good if I rested on my laurels. He outplayed me for the best part of four games and he could quite easily have won 3-1 at that point.

I do remember looking at his eyes at the end of the fourth. At that point I was wobbling, but he looked strong. He was the man and I knew I had to get a good start in the fifth, which thankfully I did. Chris Robertson, the England coach who was in my corner, had some words of wisdom. He told me that I 'would have taken 2-2 five weeks ago, so put it all out there'.

Weirdly I visualised every round and what the score would be. In the final I saw it as 3-2 to me so I was prepared for it. The tension started to be relieved as the fifth progressed, my short game returned and I started to stretch James to the front. Suddenly, the back corners became more open and it was one of the best fifth games I have ever played in my career.

Yes, there have been other thrilling battles, not least with James. But this topped everything. It wasn't just a case of it being a great match, it was the backstory we had both been through. The fact we did ourselves proud on the biggest stage in our sport. Hearing Jerusalem on the podium. Over a million people having watched on the BBC. Over 2,000 watching live. There's no doubt that this was the highlight of my career.

How Nick Matthew got back to business...

With Nick Matthew's right leg out of action following surgery, Mark Campbell's main priorities as physical conditioner were to maintain his cardiovascular strength and conditioning throughout the rest of his body. The New Zealander set about a four-week timeline to get the Englishman ready for Glasgow:

Week 1: Operation at start of week
Left leg strength
Upper body strength

Week 2: Post-operation
Left leg strength
Upper body strength
Non-involved cardiovascular work
Light bike sessions/pool sessions (physio-led)
Squash movement patterns (squatting and split squatting) (physio-led)
Light isolated single leg strength on the involved leg

Week 3
Left leg strength
Upper body strength
Non-involved CV work
Aerobic conditioning bike sessions and pool sessions
Squash movement patterns (squatting and split squatting) (physio-led)
Light isolated single leg strength on the involved leg
Light static hitting on court (physio-led)
Light squash court movement (ghosting) (physio-led)

Week 4
Leg strength
CV conditioning
Ghosting and squash movement patterns (physio-led)
Court sessions with static hitting/ghosting
Solo court work
Coached hitting/feeding session
Progressive hitting to match play (vs local club professional)
Full match play by the final day of this week (Sunday vs Alister Walker)

Eyewitness: How the *Daily Telegraph* saw it...

There was a certain uniformity on the podium at the conclusion of the men's singles programme: Englishmen took a clean sweep of gold, silver and bronze medals.

But anyone who believes animosity is solely dictated by national boundaries would have been disabused by what happened in the sedate surroundings of Glasgow's elegant West End.

What a match there was for the gold medal at the Scotstoun sports centre. Across 100 minutes of heft and graft, thrash and swat, the world champion Nick Matthew and James Willstrop, the former world No. 1, battling toe to toe, the sweat washing across the court.

Theirs was not simply a scrap for posterity. This was personal.

'There is antagonism,' Willstrop said. 'We're very disparate characters.'

Let us put it this way: off the court, the pair may be team-mates but they are not friends. And on it, they really went to war.

Through five exhausting games the lead was swapped promiscuously as they appeared to take out all their mutual dislike on the small white object sharing their space. My, did they whack that ball very, very hard.

'He's so good that I can't play good squash against him. He brings out the worst in me,' Matthew said afterwards, the sweat still pouring off his nose.

'When I play him I'm reduced to caveman squash, no subtlety, just belt the ball as hard as you can.'

It may have been unreconstructed, Neanderthal stuff, but boy was it compelling. This was squash at its best: dynamic, brutal, the perfect advertisement for the game.

'I wonder how squash is not an Olympic sport,' Matthew said. 'This was the Commonwealth Games but that was a world standard final.

'I hope the IOC are watching and think, "Wow we need to get this sport in." Because I think it had everything.'

Given their preparations, it was amazing either man was able to stand, never mind deliver such sustained excitement.

Willstrop was close to pulling out of the competition with a hip problem, while Matthew had undergone knee surgery just five weeks before arriving in Glasgow. But there was no hint of either giving any quarter as they scrapped and harried and charged around the court.

The lead was swapped like the parcel at a children's party. Matthew had taken the first game (in which he had played only one winner, his opponent making 10 errors to gift him the points).

Willstrop came back with the second, then Matthew took the third. When Willstrop won an incredible rally in the 14th point of the fourth game, the momentum seemed to swing behind him.

With both men playing shots that defied all known laws of physics, trading drops and smashes, the ball switching from corner to corner, it was exhausting to watch, never mind play. Willstrop, 6ft 4in of refined power, seized his chance to send the match into a decider.

For the younger man it seemed a defining moment. He had not beaten his heated rival since 2007; he lost to him in the final of the last Commonwealth Games in Delhi.

Now he thought he was genuinely in with a chance. But, tenacious, athletic, strong as he was, he was ultimately let down by mistakes.

As tiredness began to constrict his movements, an unforced error when he sliced the ball into the tin when well placed at the front of the wall gave Matthew a 7-3 lead in the final game.

Another to go 8-4 down when he hit the ball out of the court altogether was as bad. And a third on 9-4 effectively finished him. Though it was Matthew's skill that ultimately decided things. Poor Willstrop ended up on his face, sliding forlornly into the corner, having first thrown his racket in vain pursuit of a beautifully flighted lob by the champion.

Matthew celebrated by dashing out of the court to the stands to kiss his pregnant partner, Esme, on the stomach.

'We're having a baby in a couple of weeks, so I better make the most of this because it will no longer be the best moment of my life then,' he said with a smile.

But that was not before he acknowledged the supreme effort the challenger had given, wrapping his arms round the vanquished man and congratulating him on his contribution to the 11-9, 8-11, 11-5, 6-11, 11-5 defeat.

'He's a superb competitor,' Matthew said of his rival. 'I'm from Yorkshire, I'm an only child and I'm a Leo, so I'm a stubborn so-and-so. And I needed to be out there.'

18

Ramy's Resurrection

Ramy Ashour (Egypt)
2014 World Championship Final, Doha
Beat Mohamed Elshorbagy 13-11, 7-11, 5-11,
11-5, 14-12

IN 2013 I became the first Egyptian winner at the British Open since the 1960s. It was a victory against some tough conditions and hard circumstances I was facing back home with the revolution in Cairo. It will forever live loud and clear in my memory because it wasn't only a victory against a great player like Greg Gaultier, but more for me.

I know that the BBC did a story around the same time asking if I was the greatest rackets player ever. For me, it's really nothing special. It's brilliant that people say those things and I have always been a believer of praise and criticism. I have to enjoy the moment when something great is said about you. But I can't think too much about myself, there are too many good players on the tour. I wanted to stay where I am mentally and not get caught out by the good words. But, yes, it does give you confidence.

When everything came together in my game I started to become more creative in my squash. There is a strategy which I tailor for myself, something that works for you. I never copied from someone. I tried to find work-outs that are best for me and it doesn't necessarily have to work for other people. It's more about individual habits and to be open to new ideas, listening to the young and old.

Jansher Khan was my idol because of his technique and the way he plays; Jahangir Khan for his personality, his game and everything about him. I haven't had the chance to be with Jansher as much but I know how humble and giving Jahangir is. He just wants to give out his advice the whole time. And for me, just as it was with Jahangir, it's how to be physically consistent and dedicated over those years. Squash is not a day job, it's a hard lifestyle.

So I wanted to show the squash world that you can be creative. The more you love this game the more you have to try new things for yourself.

People think I'm doing something magical, but it's not the fitness or routine. I will never be more professional than players like Nick [Matthew] or James [Willstrop], as they have been doing this for their whole lives and it's the way they have been raised.

I do most of the normal things: footwork, cardio, weights and strength. I have always given 100 per cent but I was never that knowledgeable about myself or the way I train, until I started getting injuries.

When I became world number one for the first time in 2010 I started to get some injuries in the major tournaments. I had to concede matches during the 2010 and 2011 World Championships and I knew I had to do something about it.

I started to have a relationship with the Aspire Academy in Qatar. I had to learn about conditioning and my body as a whole. I had to start reading and speaking and working with people who knew about these problems.

But I started to have problems again in 2014 and it turned out that my last match before the World Championships in Doha was the British Open in May.

I had a major tear in my hamstring that was detected by a doctor in New York. There was a 30cm tear in my hamstring that had been there for about three years. It had flared up and then healed every time. So for all that time, my body had been adapting and had been extremely clever! But because it had been working so hard, at some point it cracked up.

I was recommended to have some therapy treatment called PRP (platelet-rich plasma) therapy, which rearranges blood cells and re-injects into your body to generate a speedier recovery. The treatment helped with the healing. Instead of taking seven to eight months, it took two and a half. What makes it great is that there is no chemical, it's your own blood that's been treated and re-injected. It's not intrusive and the doctor told me because it had almost healed I could play the World Championships.

Ninety per cent of the doctors said that it didn't work. But I said during the tournament that we would see at the end of the week who was right. It had been a long journey after nearly three months of treatment in New York.

I had four types of people saying different things in the build-up to Doha. I had supportive people, placid people, negative and positive people. The positive people believed I could really win the world title and I could feel their energy. I know it's different from someone who just says it and someone who really believes I can make it. It was an interesting time; all the effort I was putting into trying to be fit for the World Championships and thinking about it all day, every day. I asked myself, 'Is this really going to work?'

You develop mentally as you get older but I am not sure about my physical side. You are supposed to develop physically over your peak times, but I have been grinding away since I was 11! In Egypt, what we are good at is pushing ourselves until we collapse. It is what I have been doing since those early years. It has been about killing yourself on court and working as hard as you can.

In that respect, my peak years were from about 14 until I was 21. I then started to get problems with my ankles, my feet and hamstrings. I think I am now at my peak mentally; looking back at what I've done with the least amount of resources, regarding support and my body, it's something that I can't think about too much.

Having not tested myself properly on court, I was worrying so much in the three months leading up to Qatar, that by the time it got to the stage of actually playing, there was nothing more that I could do. There would be matches in the past when I was hesitant, stressed and pressurised, where all the negative thoughts I had stored up would resurface.

It was like all the energy that had been locked in all those months was being released. But my main objective in Doha was to stay healthy. Win or lose, I wanted to finish it injury free. If I could achieve that then I would be happy.

But to come back and play was always going to be one of my biggest battles. It was like I was challenging ten people inside my head the whole time. You get put into certain situations you have to face and rise up to; otherwise you will end up at the bottom. It's not what I wanted.

I was drawn against Ivan Yuen, of Malaysia, in the first round. It was my first match in six months, but it wasn't about one match, or one victory, it was a sequence of matches and a matter of consistency.

I had a lot in my head during the match. I tried to stay in the zone and block the thoughts out. I just tried to keep it simple. I said to myself that if it worked out in the week, it will mean that they were right. If it didn't go that well, then I would try another way.

It's always been a mental battle for me on the court, and my second round was no exception. Englishman Adrian Grant is not an easy opponent at all. If you get sucked into his game, he puts the pressure on you big time. Haitham Effat, the Egyptian coach, just told me to keep imposing my game, from the first point to the last point. It was all about having that mental lock.

I then enjoyed my matches with Miguel Rodriguez and Borja Golan. With Miguel, you just cannot move slowly, it's just impossible. I love the way he plays – he is unique, he has got a completely different perspective on the ball, while you learn a lot of subtleties watching him play. I knew we were going to have a great match. His logic towards the ball is just like nobody else on tour.

Borja is also pushing all the top guys. He is so strong, is such an amazing athlete and is a threat to all the other players. I really enjoyed it and even though I was 2-0 down I didn't think about nicks or winners, I just tried to find the right strategy that would make me win.

There are days where you are in a dark place and you've got to get yourself to a brighter place. In life, you seem to have hurdles in your way. But if you overcome these tests you get more of an edge, more confidence out of it.

And I took a lot of confidence from the Golan match as now it was up to face Greg in the semi-final. I knew there that our first game was crucial. I thought it would actually go on forever and forever: it was back and forth, back and forth and I'm glad it went my way. He was desperate to get it. I could feel how desperate he was and I understood that because I arrived from nowhere – and he deserved it more than me.

But on the other hand, I had been through a lot. So I went on there, fought for every point and made sure I gave 100 per cent. I had to make sure that, deep inside, I would give all that I could and push away all the demons.

Of course I had in my mind the fact that Greg had never won a world title after being in so many finals. I knew that he had been preparing well for this. But

I had been through a lot to get here and my thinking was that I had to give 100 per cent to make it.

I couldn't think of anything negative surrounding Greg. He wanted to eat me and I wanted to eat him in our semi-final, but it wasn't a vicious thing! We are good friends off court and I knew that if I played well and won he would be happy for me and the same if it was the other way around. We are professional enough both on and off court.

I got through the match. The hours afterwards were hard, knowing I was in the world final. I was thinking a lot. Sometimes when you get that far, you start to think in a different way. My aim was to try and stay balanced, think about safety first and look ahead at trying to win.

In my semi-final I picked up a shoulder niggle in the last couple of points against Greg. And it came back into play in the first game against Mohamed the next day in the final when I went to play an overhead backhand shot.

I am very conscious of my body and I know what works best. Rod Whiteley, a sports physiotherapist working at Aspetar Sports Medicine Hospital in Doha, was trying to ease up the pain before and during the final, though I knew exactly what the problem was. It was almost as if I was trying to coach him as well! But he was great and was guiding me through the pain in between games. To have the physio there was so important, to have someone who was flexible enough to listen to you.

After the first, I couldn't seem to lift the racket. I was trying to tweak the ball around, trying to hit it differently and softly. I gripped the racket right from the top, changed my swing and still it wasn't working.

So I just tried to move it around and mix up the pace until I could buy myself more time. I played through the pain barrier.

It was getting to the point, even so early in the final, where I was thinking, 'You know what, if I have to do surgery after this match then I don't care!' You don't get to be in a world final every day and this was my mindset at this point. I was desperate for it. I had to push through the pain and see what came out the other side. I gave it my all and it kind of loosened a bit.

Mohamed took the next two games to lead 2-1. I knew then how hard it was going to be to beat him. You have to be so structured and disciplined every time you play him. He also plays at such a high pace that you have to live with that too. I like his style, I love the way he plays and it's great for the game that he is pushing the bar, not only for me but for the sport.

I wouldn't say that it's true that I don't have a game plan where it gets to the stage when I am playing within myself. Like it was in 2012 when we played the world final, the atmosphere was electrifying. We actually came out on Harley Davidson bikes that night, two years previously. The idea wasn't mine, it was compere Robert Edwards's idea. It was quite weird, yet it added to all the energy in the Khalifa Sports Complex.

Mohamed was really on it in the second and third games. In the fourth, we played some really brutal rallies. I could see him gritting his teeth like he didn't want to leave until it was done. He was crawling around me.

It was like a fight in the fifth, both of us trying to get into each other's game. We were both trying to produce the best of our best squash. He is explosive, smart and had his strategies and plans. You have to keep thinking while you are playing him and you can't stay complacent for one second.

You can't hit a loose shot too, as he will string together too many points in a row. He pushes me and motivates me and does the same to all the top-ten players. I'm not the oldest guy, but he is younger than us and he has been bursting through the ranks.

Playing and winning the 2012 final against him was definitely on my mind: same player, same round, same venue, same tournament, same title. But two years on this was a different mentality. His game had developed into one where he had become world number one heading into the worlds. And God bless him. In 2012, it had been the other way around.

There were some quality rallies and we were both doing a lot of thinking on court in a bid to break the other. It really was an electric atmosphere now.

It is what we live for: to play a great shot, or you come that close in a match and you hear the crowd going. You never know when it's all going to end, so you have to appreciate it and understand the surroundings. Some players don't like the noise and managing your focus in the box can be hard to deal with sometimes, that's for sure. Coming out successfully in a big match is a big deal, especially when you're trying to make the people happy!

I just tried not to think too positively or negatively so I wouldn't get my hopes too high or my expectations too low. I knew I was trying to just embrace all the thoughts and plug them all in.

It was nerve-racking holding those five match balls. I am absolutely sure that every time I got a match point, he was thinking that he was about to be the world champion having led the match. But it was the same for me. It was hard for the both of us.

Squash at the best of times feels like a boxing match in that small glass court. Sometimes it feels like such a contentious vibe – not in a bad way – but in a way that everyone is on the edge of their seats in suspense in the match. You are secluded inside the four glass walls.

At the same time, the energy and the way the crowd connect and give their attention to you makes you want to live the moment. No one knows what is going to happen and we're no less than tennis in that respect when you watch some of those great finals.

I remember a lot of people telling me right after the match and in the weeks that followed that my nerves almost cracked. But these types of matches don't happen often and that is what makes squash so unique in so many different ways.

It was a total relief when, after getting through the trauma of losing those match points, I finally got over the winning line. It was a dream come true. It took me a while for it to sink in and look back – I could never watch the match again, it would be too much! – on all I have done and been through; the times of losing hope, getting it all back and making sure nothing was going to happen to my leg and seeing myself limping out like I did the previous year in Manchester.

It had been a risk to come to the States. Life is not the easiest there, but it is definitely a better atmosphere to train. It was a good choice. It was a great venture and I am grateful to God that I was strong enough to make it through. With all those things, the Doha win was the most special ever for me.

I arrived back in Cairo a few days later and there was a big reception at the airport. There were TV, magazine and newspaper interviews to do and it was the first time I saw such media celebrations, much more so than my first world title in 2008 and the British Open victories.

I know that Amr Shabana took the back door out of the airport when there was a mass of media waiting after one of his world titles. But Amr has his own way and no one can say anything about it as he is a four-time world champion. He is such a legend and the way he deals with and handles things is what has made him what he is.

But I'm okay with the media. We may be a little disappointed with them when it comes to squash as they are only interested in soccer and team aspects, rather than individual sports. For me, it is getting people to understand the sport more – that this game is such a pleasure to watch once you get into it. It's why the Olympics is such a big deal for us and getting the world to understand how much squash could grab people's attention.

I just really want to get the sport out there to show how beautiful it is. For me, squash is more about how disciplined you can be. It teaches you discipline and commitment, self-respect, humility – all of which you can use in your social life. It's not just about entertaining and being healthy, it's more about the lifestyle. It is mentally very tough so to stay consistent and be strong mentally is important. If you can do this on and off the court it will change your perspective on your social life as well.

The only getaway in my life is winning. Other players can get away with losing and cope. For me, it is black. You learn a lot from it. I don't know why it is like this. Maybe it's because I work too hard and put a lot of pressure on myself. People think life is so good, but it will be a lot worse for me personally, if I don't win. I am constantly fighting battles both on and off court.

I am my own psychologist. I know I am good analyst. I observe a lot and the more I grow up, the more I learn and what I should do to stay constant and consistent in my lifestyle.

A lot of players have raised the bar. Everyone has their own game. Australians play like the Egyptians, the Egyptians play like the English. Players are integrating other schools of thought into their play. It makes it harder for everyone, especially as players can last two hours on court now.

I'd love to keep playing for as long as I can. I love the effort and I love being tired. I've always thought about sport a bit differently and I've always loved the idea that in what I do, it makes me appreciate the very simple things in life: water, air and food. Any kind of food!

Playing squash makes you appreciate these positive things. It doesn't make you think about the luxuries in life. I just love the simplicity of it all.

What Mohamed Elshorbagy said in defeat

I gave it everything I had. When it's 2-2 and 10-10, it's all about luck and you can't do much about it. I didn't do anything wrong and he just played a super shot at the end.

It was his best performance of the whole tournament and it was the best performance I could have given. I said in my interview before the match that if there was someone there to stop me from winning it was going to be Ramy.

But if someone was going to stop Ramy, then it was going to be me. It was 50-50 and could have gone either way. The only thing that didn't go right was letting the first game go when I was 8-4 up. It was a very important opening game.

Matches like these you don't forget. It is important for me to have Ramy on tour. He is the only player who can push me over my limits. I was getting some balls back in that match that I never would have envisaged getting back in my whole life.

The way the pace was played by the both of us was the kind of pace we only play against each other. We definitely push each other and it's so important for the game to have him there.

It's a great rivalry between us. It's a very fair one and it will be exciting for the sport over the next few years. It is the respect we have for each other. We both know that after those long rallies that they are crazy. They are only played when we play each other. Two years previously we had similar rallies in the world final. This time we had even more of them. We gave it everything.

If Ramy was going to lose in the event, it had to be in the early rounds. That was when he might not have been at his most confident. In his match against Gaultier, it gave him the confidence to play like he did in the final.

Seven months out and to come back to win the tournament? It was incredible.

Eyewitness: With a world title at stake in Qatar, *Squash Player*'s Ian McKenzie witnessed the most dramatic match in squash history

Resurrection!

If Ramy Ashour now announced that he was going to walk on water, a bunch of believers would gather to witness it, as he could probably do it.

How else can you explain the Egyptian coming back from six months on the sidelines – that is six months in the most brutal of racket sports, where the best athletes are training daily and picking their events to build to a physical, mental and competitive peak – to capture the world title for a third time?

Ashour, you may remember, succumbed to injury in the last World Championship in Manchester, where he withdrew against Nick Matthew in the semi-finals. In the British Open he lost to Greg Gaultier in the semi-finals and had not competed since. This was the sport's 'fruitcake', plagued by injury and dogged by accusations that half of the problem was mental. Compete in Doha? Ridiculous!

It was even audacious to turn up and face Matthew, looking for a fourth world title; the brilliant Gaultier, cursed after four world title defeats, but who would give anything to win one; Mohamed Elshorbagy, who claimed he had the pace to blow them all away; and the exquisite maestro, four-time champion Amr Shabana, waiting for them all to slip up. What was Ashour doing here?

The whispers and hard-nosed assessments were that he would pull out again as he eased past Malaysian qualifier Ivan Yuen after just winning the second game 14-12, beat English veteran Adrian Grant in three and defeated the Colombian 'rubberball', Miguel Angel Rodriguez, in four. Ashour was playing his exhibition squash, the observers said, just wait until he gets a really tough match.

Then, in the quarter-finals, against Borja Golan he stumbled as the Spaniard, with nothing to lose, hit brilliant form to take the first game. In a fluctuating battle, Ashour looked slow at times and guessed at other times, but won through in four as the chants of the faithful – 'RAM-ME, RAM-ME, RAM-ME' – rang throughout the Khalifa Complex.

Still there was the prevalent view that the Egyptian magician couldn't go much further, for how could he live with Gaultier's pace or Elshorbagy's? You can't just turn up to play your first event for six months (not just any event but the World Championship) and expect to compete at that pace. Ridiculous!

And so to the top-seeded Gaultier, who had come through in four hard games against Egyptian Omar Mosaad in the last 16 and then overpowered Cameron Pilley, the Australian who was thrilled to make the quarter-finals.

Compere Robert Edwards helpfully reminded the Frenchman of his past failures as he warmed up against Ashour in the semi-finals. And what an exquisite encounter it was. Matches are generally won and lost on mistakes. Not this one. Gaultier hit 10 outright winners – which the best shot-reader in the sport could not even get to when he dived – and committed just four mistakes (one tin, one mishit, one forced error and one stroke) in 34 minutes of searing pace.

Ashour made just five errors, but his 13 wonderful, mesmerising winners helped him claim the first game 17-15. In diving, though, he had injured his already-taped elbow and had to take an injury break. As he left the court at the end of the game, Gaultier thumped his own elbow and pointed at the referee. It is a moot point whether Ashour's injury was an existing one or not, but this was a beautiful game without doubt. The demons in Gaultier's head then gifted the next two games and the match to Ashour, with his collapse encapsulated in his performance in the third game, where he made eight mistakes and hit only one winner in crashing 11-5 in only seven minutes.

So Ashour was through to the final, where he faced Elshorbagy, whose pace, as he had predicted, had been too much for Matthew, after the English title holder had squeezed past India's Saurav Ghosal – who took time to come on to his game, but then challenged mightily – in four and Shabana, who started poorly to scupper his chance of repeating his US Open victory over Matthew.

Elshorbagy, meanwhile, had triumphed in a ding-dong battle of the big hitters against Germany's Simon

Rosner in four, then beat South African Stephen Coppinger (who had taken out English eighth seed Daryl Selby in the first round and Egyptian no.10 seed Tarek Momen in the last 16 to make the quarters for the first time) in a creditable three.

The Final

There was a nervous start to the all-Egyptian final, with Elshorbagy racing into a 5-1 lead after two minutes on the back of three Ashour errors and then surging 9-4 ahead, but the 23-year-old second seed could not build the consistent pressure he imposed on Matthew.

Ashour pushed the ball like a table tennis player, snapped at it early, rolled it softly, mixed the pace, held and flicked it so that the world number one rarely knew where to run to next. Then Ashour found the nick and the points began to mount as even the fastest man in the world could not run these balls down. Ashour surged through, twisting and turning Elshorbagy, to take the first game 13-11.

Strangely, the fourth seed was more reticent in the second game and, in old-fashioned terms, slow-balled. He did not take one full swing at the ball, pushed and prodded at it brilliantly to edge ahead 7-6, wriggling his shoulder as he tried to find the least painful way of hitting the ball (throughout the match Ashour had physio and spray treatment on his shoulder between games and raced back to the court so as not to earn a conduct penalty). He lost that game 11-7 and the third 11-5. Some thought he would not continue. His prospects seemed bleak.

However, the 27-year-old then launched one of the most incredible comebacks the game has ever seen. Exquisite lobs, volley lobs and clinging balls all deprived Elshorbagy of pace. Ashour's retrievals and winners seemed to defy the law of physics and were accompanied by a cacophony of cheers, oohs, aahs and the chant of 'RAM-ME, RAM-ME, RAM-ME'. The two-time champion drew level by winning the fourth 11-5.

The pain in the shoulder was still there; it just had to be endured now. Both players fired balls into their opponent's body, only for them to be parried away behind their backs to gasps of astonishment. Then, as if possessing magical powers, Ramy stormed clear from 5-5 in the fifth game to match ball at 10-5. He was on the verge of a comeback rare in sport and proving that miracles do happen. He needed just one point to finish the match, which shouldn't have been a problem for a genius in this form.

However, Elshorbagy got one point back with a fine backhand volley drop winner. Then another and another and another and another. 'No let', 'I got the ball on the racket' complained Ramy. It was suddenly 10-10. What was happening?

Then Elshorbagy's strings broke and so we had a sixth match ball for Ashour. A video review, a no-let, upheld to a deafening background chant – 'RAM-ME, RAM-ME, RAM-ME'. A stroke followed, when Ashour played an awkward ball he didn't have to, so now it was Elshorbagy's chance. A perfect dying straight ball saved it, though.

Elshorbagy stopped mid-rally to get the court wiped and a there was at last a chance to catch one's breath. So far there had been six match balls for Ashour and one for Elshorbagy.

A 'no-let' penalising Ashour followed, but it was overruled. He backed it up with an unplayable winning drop and suddenly the referee was announcing, 'Match to Ashour, 13-11, 7-11, 5-11, 11-5, 14-12.' And a world title. What a comeback, what a return – in fact, it was nothing less than a resurrection.

Ashour bent over and hugged himself for a long time, leapt in the air, prayed, lay quietly in a fetal position and waved to the chanting fans. 'EGYPT, EGYPT, EGYPT' rang out the chant in Arabic. Have there ever been scenes like this at a squash match?

'I'm speechless, it's unbelievable,' the new champion said as he blew kisses to the crowd and thanked his fitness trainer, Allistair McCaw, and physiotherapists Rod Whitley and James Hashimoto.

Yes, we thought it was unbelievable too.

Index

The Players